Developing**Leaders**

46

Quarterly

MAKING ORGANIZATIONS MORE HUMAN

Who Cares?
The Power of Compassionate Leadership

Catalyzing your leadership practice

Edited by Roland Deiser and Roddy Millar

Publisher's note

IEDP Ideas for Leaders Ltd
42 Moray Place, Edinburgh, EH3 6BT
www.ideasforleaders.com

in association with the Center for the Future of Organization at the
Drucker School of Management
www.futureorg.org

Publishers: Roland Deiser and Roddy Millar
Editor-in-Chief: Roddy Millar
Senior Editor: Roland Deiser
Associate Editors: Saar Ben-Attar (Africa), Suzie Lewis (Europe)
Conrado Schlochauer (LatAm), Ravi Shankar (SE Asia)
Art Direction: Nick Mortimer – nickmortimer.co.uk

Copyright ©2025 IEDP Ideas for Leaders Ltd and contributors

ISBN 978-1-91-552943-5 (Paperback)
ISBN 978-1-91-552944-2 (e-Pub)
ISSN 2044-2203 (Developing Leaders Quarterly)

www.developingleadersquarterly.com

Contents

Who Cares? This issue's theme is on the role of care and compassion in leadership, and we ask this question not just as a pun, but because this theme is often pushed down organizational priorities as it seems too 'soft' or unrelated to the bottom line. This attitude is even more prevalent in the current political climate.

Creating a sense that employees matter. That they are more than just cogs in a system. These are vital ingredients for all leaders to know how to deploy. We are cogs (without whom the system would run less effectively) but importantly we are living ones, with lives of our own and family and ideas and things that motivate us beyond work. These concepts are at the heart of human-centred leadership – and paying attention to these facts, so that all an organization's staff and external stakeholders feel they matter - consistently shows improved organizational performance and productivity over the medium to long-term.

You can sweat your organization only for a short period, before cracks appear and energy lapses. That may well be in the interests of the short-term manager, but it is never in the interests of the leader looking to sustain performance over an extended period.

This issue explores these themes. And – as probably all our content will do for the foreseeable future – we have to see much of this through the prism of AI. The daily changes that AI, both analytic and generative, is bringing to the workplace is going to impact how we lead (see our book reviews for a glimpse into these themes too).

We start off with a broad piece from **Suzie Lewis**, who surveys the conditions where we try to create change from in organizations, and the power that compassionate, human-centred leadership can foster in transforming systems. **Michelle Holliday**, the author and 'thrivability maven' takes this concept forward with her examination of organizations as living systems and how we need to nurture them and their constituents to manage today's complexity and stress.

Our next two articles dive into empathy and self-compassion, with wonderful pieces by empathy advocate **Maria Ross**, and London Business School faculty and author **Kirstie Drummond Papworth**.

Meena Kumar gives us her insightful piece in an article titled Care is Cure, which encapsulates so much of this issue. And **Judith Parke** rounds-up our care and compassion articles with a deeper and more practical dive down the thread that is woven through all the articles on psychological safety.

As always, we offer more tangential and distinct pieces from the issue theme too. **Samir Selmanović**, shines a light on the monomyth of the Hero's Journey narrative, and shares with us a newer alternative narrative for today's more complex world.

With a strong eye on the importance of supporting and developing leaders across organizations and at all levels, I am delighted to have **Elana Friedman** writing a powerful piece on middle managers, and the importance of creating role clarity to enable the conditions for them to do their best work.

We close with two different pieces. The first from **Hamilton Mann**, which connects to our previous issue on AI more concretely, with his discourse on Artificial Integrity. And **Orit Wolf's** article on how we overlook core artistic skills and competencies at our peril, like enabling and championing disruption, experimentation and visualizing through alternative eyes, in our more transactionally bounded organizations – and how we need to bring these approaches ore into the mainstream.

If you would like to share your thoughts and comments with us on any of these articles, or have thoughts on future areas we might cover, we are always delighted to hear from our readers. Contact me at editor@dl-q.com.

Roddy Roland

Roddy Millar, Editorial Director and Co-publisher
Roland Deiser, Co-publisher

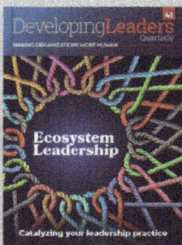

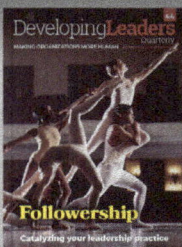

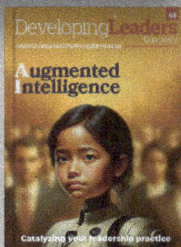

Thinking imprinted.

The first step in leadership development is creating space for reflection on your practice.

Studies show we absorb information better from print, which allows focused, uninterrupted reading and the ability to jot down thoughts.

To embed the change, Developing Leaders Quarterly is best in print. The print edition is conveniently sized to slip into your pocket, bag, or briefcase, making it easy to read in spare moments—whether commuting, at the airport, or before a meeting.

By Suzie Lewis

From Compete and Compare to Collaborate and Care

One of the biggest shifts that leaders must manage in the digital age is from ego to eco – the Achilles heel of adaptive and conscious leadership. It sounds simple but is very difficult to embody as we know that so much of human behaviour is driven by ego, and so much of what happens in organizational culture, too.

Yet this shift from ego to eco is in full swing and becoming more and more pressing in today's organizational ecosystems, particularly in the operational workspace. We still depict organizational design in linear and binary organization charts. And we still believe in the myth that these represent the authority, hierarchy and power dynamics of an organization – except that they don't.

Organizations as Living Systems

Organizations are complex living systems that house several layers of relationships, assumptions, hidden hierarchies, and power dynamics that are very real but never formalized or acknowledged. They are, however, embodied as 'the way we do things around here.' This echoes the deeper layer of implicit assumptions as per Ed Schein's model of organizational culture: the job titles used, the dress code or other 'artifacts' as the first visible signs of the culture. Then espoused values – things an organization says about its culture and ways of working (vision/mission statements, value statements, team charters, etc.) – which are deeper indicators and levers of culture than artifacts, but still shallower than underlying beliefs. And, finally, underlying assumptions about how people should work together, what is accepted practice or what behaviours will really lead to workplace success or failure.

For example, many organizations use job-sharing to give flexibility and equity, yet employees may feel that people in job shares are not considered for a promotion as readily as those who are not. These complex relationships, dynamics and interdependencies are by their very nature implicit and non-linear, and such a systemic view is key if leaders are to intentionally create a culture where everyone can thrive.

It is not about 'what the system allows you to do', but about how you intentionally design and redesign the system to allow people and the culture to evolve.

Today, we remain essentially focused on the individual in terms of performance management, reward and recognition. Organizational processes and policies also remain essentially focused on the individual. The existing processes and implicit assumptions and codes of organizational culture are recognized patterns in the system and will not be changed as long as they are rewarded and validated by the system. Quite the opposite in fact: they will become more ingrained as long as we do not break the patterns. This is the same for all types of practices and habits that feed the leadership culture of an organization.

I have had so many discussions with leaders about inclusive practices and using the diversity we have (or don't have) to innovate or create a high performing team. We regularly discuss making sure each voice is heard but we do not talk about how we change the system in which these voices think, act and interact. It would be

Authentic and courageous conversations are the key to creating the conditions for collaboration, care and inclusion to happen.

far better to adapt the system, which is the bigger, harder and more sustainable bet. We must look at exactly where biases and assumptions lie, what is implicitly accepted and rewarded and what we can do about it. It is a continuous process that requires a consistent effort from leadership, ongoing dialogue, and individual agency. It is not about 'what the system allows you to do', but about how you intentionally design and redesign the system to allow people and the culture to evolve.

The Conundrum of Polarities

This is the dialectic conundrum in today's digital world – constantly navigating the extremes of two conflicting paradigms, such as individual vs. collective, control vs. empowerment, or knowing vs. learning. For example, I recently worked with a leader who was willing to experiment and 'let things emerge', but in the same breath asked me to prove that it would work before trying. Not only is this a tall order; it also exemplifies the conundrum of wanting to try but not feeling safe enough to do so. We need to find a way of navigating these polarities to create a space where you have collaboration not competition, where you have accountability and collective responsibility, and where you can have high performance and courageous conversations. After all, you cannot have one without the other – you cannot have high performance and thriving teams without courageous conversations and a culture of care.

Can you recall an occasion on which you were trying to get other people on your side, trying to influence and create a space where things could happen? The lever for this is to have conversations that are meaningful, deeper, uncomfortable, courageous, sometimes difficult and incredibly impactful. The quality of collaboration depends on the quality of the conversations, and authentic conversations are the key to creating the conditions for collaboration, care and inclusion to happen.

This then begs the question of how we bring about these conditions. Leaders must be able to define and make these choices and move from a passive stance to an active stance so that they can start visualizing and designing what this environment could look like. Some helpful questions to ask might be: What skills do I need? How can I equip my peers and teams to start with the hard inner work and then move out to a more collective design of how we collaborate more efficiently?

It is important to understand the 'what is' and the 'what isn't' in this space, to get curious, and to speak to people by engaging in authentic and courageous conversations. We must look at the environment from a lens of empathy and care as well and ask ourselves: What mindsets are present here? What are the unwritten assumptions and biases? Do I ask people what they are really feeling and take their answers into account? Do I regularly challenge myself and my perspectives openly with my peers and teams?

We worked together with an SME for 12 months looking to build a Diversity, Equity and Inclusion strategy. However, as we delved into the topic, we created a systemic view by linking innovation, employee engage-

ment, performance, talent retention and ultimately competitive advantage to the leadership and culture needed to create the conditions for people to thrive and innovate. In other words, we were creating a culture of care. We worked to intentionally create systemic change and design the relevant systems and processes for the new behaviours to be rewarded. This was, of course, a journey, not a one-month project.

We started by questioning the status quo and the implicit assumptions through feedback and dialogue on the lived experiences of both leaders and employees. This assessment of the existing culture, processes and systems allowed us to use the building blocks that were already contributing to creating the environment.

A culture of care will create a safe space where individuals can be both their individual selves yet also contribute and collaborate to the bigger collective vision.

We defined what a culture of care was for them and conducted mass awareness exercises across the different parts of the organization to determine how this translated into their everyday rituals and operations. This was an iterative process that enabled us to pilot how to create higher-quality conversations and dialogue in the organization. Engagement scores rose by 12% and powerful communities started to take root.

A culture of care will create a safe space where individuals can be both their individual selves yet also contribute and collaborate to the bigger collective vision with a longer-term perspective. However, leaders will often focus on what is easy to see and fix, rather than investing time and effort in uncovering the deeper systemic issues, i.e., they tend to address the symptoms rather than the root cause. The constant pressure on delivering results, exacerbated by silo culture, adds fuel to the ego mindset: that the focus on 'this is my budget,' or 'that's the objective for my area,' or 'my team has the best results' often leads to blame, pressure, and short-sighted competitive battles.

These are all important and performing parts of a disjointed whole. We must encourage a wider, more holistic view, with a collective that is made up of thriving individuals who collaborate towards a common goal, instead of individuals striving to be the best and deliver the most, for essentially their personal gain and recognition.

This is not just a human-centered ideal. More than ever in today's complex world we do not have all the answers. It is hard to admit that we do not know it all, that maybe we are wrong and that maybe we are sorry for the way we reacted, but it is essential for learning and progress. Apologizing or admitting failure is not about making the other person right or beating yourself up. Saying sorry means that you value your relationship more than your ego. Admitting failure means choosing learning over knowing. It means that you value growth more than your ego. And herein lies the key for leading collectively.

So, how do we evolve to enable people to develop and grow, to enable a culture in which people feel nurtured and valued, where people can bring their full potential to work and in which innovation can thrive?

Conscious Inclusion for Collaboration and Care

Weaving the tapestry of care and compassion is a real leadership challenge for all organizations. How do we connect the dots through trust, empathy and with enough clarity and accountability to land in this space of care and collaboration? This is one of the biggest transformational challenges for organizations today, whether the culture is deliberately designed for this or not.

If it is not, the impact is huge because the culture becomes very toxic and can disable rather than enable performance, both individually and collectively. It can also be very demotivating: People fail to see why they should be following a particular course of action, nor do they see the value of what they are doing. Consequently, well-being and motivation decrease, and people can feel paralyzed by the unwritten yet prevalent codes of the culture. People silently obey these codes and adhere to the politics that are at play within the different systems and management models and often suffer in silence.

This is where inclusive systems help. They foster unity and care rather than uniformity, and they make the landscape more transparent and safer for people. The good news is that there is much more scope in organizations today. We see an increasing awareness of the dynamics of complex networks. We see transformational initiatives that create bottom-up momentum. We see a shift towards more holistic end-to-end processes, and we see a shift towards implementing different ways of working to harness collective wisdom. This creates a whole platform for opportunities to drive change through collaboration and care, not only in the end-to-end business processes, but also in the way we think, show up and work.

There is a reason why some organizations retain their competitive advantage, and others struggle to retain talent. Inclusion is a strategic bottom-line subject because we cannot innovate and adapt without the building blocks of consciously fostering this principle. It is not about 'being nice' or 'saying yes to everything' or 'not taking decisions', which are some of the myths I hear on a daily basis surrounding inclusion. It is about understanding who you are, holding different perspectives and scaling empathy.

Inclusive systems are by their very nature based on care. You cannot have collaborative culture without compassion – there is no one-size-fits-all as we struggle to do 'what good leaders are supposed to do.' Maybe you will never be able to take some people with you, but that is also sometimes what care may look like.

Unless we know who we are, what our patterns are, and the impact this will have on our teams, we cannot create a culture of care. Until we take the requisite distance to question our assumptions, listen to others

Inclusive systems are by their very nature based on care. You cannot have collaborative culture without compassion.

and integrate different perspectives, we cannot create a culture of care. Until we build deliberate and intentional practice to lead differently, from a place of learning, curiosity and empathy, we cannot expect our teams to do the same.

Seeing, acknowledging, and understanding system patterns is key to understanding the blueprint of how we learn and evolve. It is the basis for an intentional design of a caring environment. We must create awareness of the patterns in the system and connect people to the emotional layer of the human systems of an organization. This will help us to understand and coach collective teams not only to another way of doing, but also a different way of being. It will help us to coach the organization towards using care as a lever for systemic changes to enable this culture to take root and evolve. We therefore need to be intentional about how we go about creating these patterns of care in the system as part of the 'way we do things around here' to enable performance and well-being.

We must create awareness of the patterns in the system and connect people to the emotional layer of the human systems of an organization.

10 Principles that Foster a Culture of Care

We need to build systems of care through collaboration and healthy challenge. Building this culture of care and effective collaboration requires a focus on the following areas:

- **Human-centric approaches:** Take the time to understand your employees and their needs, and act on the moments that matter continually.
- **Leadership commitment:** Leaders must visibly and consistently express their commitment to care.

- **Trust and accountability:** Foster a culture where trust is mutual, and accountability is encouraged – leaders and employees should hold themselves accountable to the same standards of care, dignity and respect.
- **Role model inclusive practices:** Constantly check in on how included and heard people feel, if the policies and opportunities are equitable, and if people are asked how they are doing/feeling.
- **Acknowledge success and contributions:** Acknowledgement is a powerful tool for recognition and motivation that unfortunately remains little used as a lever for thriving and nurturing both individual and collective well-being and productivity.
- **Interrelationships:** Encourage understanding of the relationships and human systems of an organization.
- **Ecosystem thinking:** Encourage understanding of interconnectedness and the interrelationships between various departments, teams, and internal/external stakeholders.
- **Inclusion:** Create safe team spaces where voices matter. Do we regularly practice healthy challenge in our team? Can we express ourselves clearly? Are we intentionally developing empathy continuously as a leadership skill?

- **Collaboration:** Facilitate collaboration across boundaries (teams, departments, sites) and foster leadership where learning to collaborate is a collective responsibility and based on caring for others.
- **Sustainability:** Define an upskilling plan for all the above areas and create regenerative working models that are customized to your context and allow people to thrive.

Conclusion

Creating a culture of care in a hybrid world requires leadership, communication, and a commitment to

Encourage understanding of interconnectedness and the interrelationships between various departments, teams, and all stakeholders.

collective thinking. By focusing on intentional actions and strategies aimed at transparency, empathy, and collective accountability, organizations can create an environment where mistakes are seen as opportunities for growth, and collaboration becomes the driving force behind innovation.

With careful attention to the unique challenges of hybrid work such as communication gaps and feelings of isolation, organizations can create a more inclusive, supportive, productive and caring work culture for everyone. This transition can be especially challenging as we move into a more interconnected workspace. It also offers unique opportunities for transformation.

Suzie Lewis *is Managing Director of Transform for Value, and an executive fellow of CFFO. She was previously head of Leadership Learning at Airbus Group's Leadership Academy.*

By Michelle Holliday

Compassion and Care in Stewarding Organizational Ecologies

What role do care and compassion play in the leadership that is needed most, today and into the future?

As it stands, the prevailing concept of leadership has been characterized less by care and compassion and more by dominance and single-minded drive, guided by a worldview that frames organizations primarily as machines. But when we recognize our organizations as living ecologies, the vital role of care and compassion comes more fully into view. Purpose expands and deepens into "thrivability" – into cultivating life's ability to

Compassion and care are integrated as core strategic and collective practices, rather than incongruous add-ons to managing the machine.

thrive. Leadership is recast as stewardship, tending the conditions for system health and regenerative capacity. And compassion and care are integrated as core strategic and collective practices, rather than incongruous add-ons to managing the machine.

This evolution is essential not only for effective governance and organizational performance but for unlocking critical responses to the perils and possibilities of these times. I believe nothing could be more important.

My story

This shift in perspective and practice has been the focus of my work for the past twenty-five years, in contexts as far-ranging as tourism, life sciences, education, elder-care and agriculture. Across all of these, I offer a set of ecological principles to help people cultivate the conditions for life to thrive at every level – for themselves, for their projects and organizations as living ecosystems, for customers, community and the biosphere. Though this evolution of assumptions and habits can be disorienting or even confronting, there is also a sense of deep truth that many recognize. "What you're telling us goes against everything we've been taught for the last thirty years," said one seasoned organizational development consultant. "And at the same time, it feels like home."

What I have seen is that the intellectual and emotional stretch is well worth it, helping teams find their way to more effectiveness, more meaning, and more of what is truly needed for their own contexts and for the world. When embraced fully, this work promises remarkable outcomes in which:

- Workers and customers experience more vitality, joy, justice, learning, self-expression and self-awareness;
- The organization achieves its intended purpose creatively, gracefully and resiliently, while attracting necessary resources;

- The community discovers more connectedness, creativity, resilience and self-reliance;
- The larger ecologies we are part of are supported in their ability to be healthy and regenerative over time.

Indeed, a word I hear often in my work is "healing."

I came to this focus in my work after the disillusionment of working in brand strategy within emerging markets for two multinational companies. My sense was that something essential seemed to be missing in how – and why – we engaged customers and community. We were highly effective at manipulating people into buying something they generally didn't need and that largely didn't contribute to community wellbeing. On top of that, both companies had cultures characterized by fierce internal competition. None of it made sense to me.

In what felt like a courageous leap, I moved to a small organizational development consulting practice, working with leadership, culture and systems. And, for the most part, it felt better. But I also noticed disturbingly familiar patterns. The leaders who were our clients simply wanted us to tell them what buttons to push to get their employees to work harder for the same amount of money. It seemed a far cry from what must be possible and even needed.

Leadership is recast as stewardship, tending the conditions for system health and regenerative capacity.

Meanwhile, more of the world was waking up to persistent and worsening societal challenges, like ecological breakdown, homelessness and social division. With all of our intelligence and technological progress, I wondered why we could not solve these problems once and for all. Again, it seemed clear: something was missing in how we conceive of our role and relationships in the world.

What we are evolving beyond

This is when I started to notice a common thread across all of my experiences and observations, a particular worldview that tells us everything in the universe operates like a machine. Nowhere is this narrative more prevalent than in our understanding and practice of leadership in organizations. According to the implicit story, we are all separate from each other, separate from nature and separate from our organizations – the proverbial "cogs in the machine." We exist to compete and consume. Profitability and productivity are the things that matter most. Speed, efficiency and scale are the most effective means to those ends. More is always better. Everything can be broken down into its component parts in the interest of prediction and control. "It's not working? Re-engineer it!" "It's just business, not personal."

Within this paradigm, leadership is most often seen through the metaphors of engineering, war, or the journey. The very word "leader" comes from the Indo-European root *leith*, which means to go forth or to cross a threshold. With its assumption of linear progression, "here" is never the right place, and "there" can be known, plotted and overtaken, one milestone at a time. There is an assumption of a single all-seeing leader (or a small number of them). Leadership is a story of isolated conquerors and those who follow them.

In none of these metaphors is it clear that care and compassion have relevance or value. And so, too often, they are interpreted as a means of influence (read: manipulation) to achieve the goal of conquest and control.

This may seem like a caricature, the dominant worldview painted in its most extreme form. And rarely is this the only storyline at play. But there is strong evidence that this underlying logic has shaped every aspect of our lives, from education to healthcare to agriculture and, perhaps most of all, to business.

And of course, there is truth and value in this worldview. But there is also reason to believe that every major problem we face in society can be traced back to the limitations of that story.

An alternative perspective

Fortunately, an expanded worldview is emerging at the edges of every sector and every discipline. This story reveals the world not as a collection of simple machines and parts to be controlled but as a dynamic ecology of living systems to be tended.

In business, we see evidence of this new narrative in the growing use of terms like complexity, ecosystem, resilience, self-organization, agility and creativity – living systems concepts, all of them. We see it in the rise of impact investing, social enterprise and corporate social responsibility – explicit acknowledgements that conquest alone is an insufficient purpose and that we are not, in fact, separate from our context.

The burgeoning concept of regenerative leadership offers the latest and clearest indication of the shift; after all, only something that is alive is capable of regenerating itself. The concept has been most directly inspired by a parallel movement in agriculture, as farmers find that monoculture, factory farming and heavy use of fertilizers and machinery – that profession's equivalent of mecha-

Evidence of this new narrative in the growing use of terms like complexity, ecosystem, resilience, self-organization, agility and creativity – living systems concepts

nistic, conquest-driven leadership – steadily depletes soil fertility, diminishes nutrient density and erodes profitability. In response, there is growing acknowledgement that it is not the farmer who grows the plants, with their chemicals and heavy equipment; it is the living ecology of the soil. The farmer's more effective role is to support and participate in that local ecosystem's generative and regenerative capacity and to respond to its unique, unfolding potential. As the soil regenerates, both farm and farmer flourish. The outcome over time is a more resilient, abundant ecosystem at every level, including economically.

This is the great promise of regenerative approaches in every context, including business and community. This is what becomes possible within a worldview centred around life.

On complexity

To act on this promise, the starting point is to acknowledge more of the complexity at play. In living soil and living organizations, we find what I think of as "life's universal design principles."

- There are individual **parts**, with vital diversity of perspectives and contributions.
- There are patterns and structures of **relationship**, with complex interdependencies in continuously unfolding process and flow.
- There are new characteristics, capabilities and needs that emerge at the level of the **whole** system.

To act on this promise, the starting point is to acknowledge more of the complexity at play.

- There is **life**, therefore there is potential that cannot be predicted or controlled but can be sensed and served with ever greater attunement and wisdom.
- **Context** plays a key role within the fundamental nestedness of all living systems.

Applying these principles in human contexts, we discover a set of corresponding strategies. To cultivate generative and regenerative capacity in our projects and organizations, we can:

- invite the divergent contributions, perspectives and **passion** of the people involved;
- hone the **practice** of relationship, collaboration and learning;
- support system-level coherence and health through shared **purpose**;
- develop our collective ability to sense and serve the **potential** that most "wants" to come to life here;
- and ground our actions in awareness of and responsiveness to **place**.

On purpose

As we actively tend to these conditions, we cultivate thrivability, supporting our organizations and communities to:

- express unique potential
- generate new forms and possibilities
- integrate ever more diverse contributions into a cohesive whole
- heal disconnections
- enable necessary endings and renewal
- become ever more at home and in harmony with context.

When we see our organizations and communities as living ecologies, this becomes the obvious purpose of our efforts: enabling ever more of life to thrive, ever more. Conquest is never the singular purpose of any system's existence. Instead, it is to participate in broad system health and to contribute to the generation of new possibilities. Everything else – every product or service, every strategy and tactic – is our unique choice of method and means to that end without end.

On stewardship

With this perspective, leadership comes to be understood more broadly as stewardship. It is less a role or a title and more a commitment to work both *in* the system

To improve the health of a system, connect it to more of itself.

and *on* the system, in the individual and collective practice of tending to the needs of parts, relationships and multiple layers of wholeness. It is offered from a stance of reverence for the life in each of us and between us, as well as for the transcendent potential that we may express together.

Importantly, there is no straight line in a living ecology, as the journey metaphor would have us believe. The goal is not simply to move from place A to place B. Instead, the steward's aim is to grow roots and become ever more integrated within a particular landscape of shared context and intention. Like the regenerative farmer tending the soil, the work is to continuously cultivate a learning ecology, growing connections and continuous feedback, creating a field of deepening wisdom from which effective action can emerge. As Margaret Wheatley advises: "To improve the health of a system, connect it to more of itself."

There is also no single leader in a living ecosystem. Instead, all the parts participate in self-organizing patterns of responsive relationship and emergent wholeness. In even the simplest of organizations, it is impossi-

ble for any one person to know everything that the system needs, to anticipate all of its potential, or to coordinate its full complexity. Stewardship is necessarily a collective practice. This is how we draw on the full intelligence of the systems we steward.

This is not to say that everyone has equal voice or status. There are always some who can see more of a system than others, either through inclination or role. They may be authorized as the primary steward of a

project or an organization, with the recognition that they derive their privileged perspective *from* the system and they are responsible *to* the system for representing that collective view. This is in contrast to the prevailing concept in which a leader acts from self-authority as if they are standing apart from the system and directing it.

Stewardship is better understood as by and for "careholders," a concept that may include future generations.

On compassion and care

Such stewardship has two primary practices at its core:

1. Continuously sensing the needs of the ecologies we form together, in the practice of active *compassion*.
2. Responding with wise, effective action, in the applied practice of *care*.

Well beyond the interpersonal kindness of a leader toward a follower, this is a shared practice of compassion and care for the wholes that we form together. Specifically, it calls for methods of convening and discernment. And it requires strategies of ongoing engagement and learning.

And well beyond shareholders or even stakeholders, stewardship is better understood as by and for "careholders," a concept that may include future generations and non-human beings and systems.

What this looks like in practice

In my work, this has looked like a municipal tourism authority reconceiving their role from "managing the tourist destination" to "cultivating the hosting community." It has involved reshaping strategy to draw businesses, citizens and government together in ongoing shared stewardship of community wellbeing. The outcome has been increased community cohesion, consistent attraction of resources and support, development of inspired offerings that serve both visitors and residents, and improved economic resilience.

It looks like the Chief Operating Officer of a fast-growing biotech company bringing together Facilities, IT, People, Finance and Legal into a unified department called "Stewardship." It has involved a two-year process of developing more connection and flow, inviting more diverse perspectives, and helping people sense and serve the needs of the whole system together. The result has been a transformation from fragmented, struggling, burned-out teams to more joy, effectiveness and adaptiveness across the whole organization, as well as the ability to attract a key contract in a challenging market.

It also looks like a large non-profit whose commitment to "caring leadership" was creating a problematic parent-child dynamic, with rising cynicism and a sense of "us and them." The response has been to nurture the philosophy and practice of shared stewardship. The result is a greater sense of mutual responsibility, new ideas for improving services and operations, and more satisfaction at work.

*When we truly
acknowledge the life in and
around us and our ability
to create the conditions for
life to thrive, new visions of
reality become apparent.*

Implications

This is the necessary near-future of governance. The promise is that every project, organization and community may become a practice ground for learning how to work with complexity, difference and change. These are vital skills for a society that is more resilient, caring and aligned with the needs and limits of the biosphere. Indeed, this is perhaps the greatest responsibility of our organizations and communities today.

As I wrote in my book, *The Age of Thrivability*:

When we truly acknowledge the life in and around us and our ability to create the conditions for life to thrive, new visions of reality become apparent: new possibilities, new goals, new priorities and new actions. In embracing the perspectives this story of thrivability offers, we become more active and intentional participants in life's process. And along the way, we find a path to richer meaning, to greater compassion, to more effective collaboration, to healthy regeneration and renewal, and to more thriving, in all senses of the word.

Ultimately, if we are to navigate increasing complexity successfully... if we are to bridge the many fragmented approaches to sustainability and corporate social responsibility... if we are to solve the persistent problems of poverty, environmental degradation and conflict... and, indeed, if our species is to survive, it is precisely such an expanded lens and inspired approach that is needed.

Michelle Holliday *is a consultant, facilitator, researcher and globally recognized thought leader on regenerative leadership. She is the author of the highly acclaimed book,* The Age of Thrivability: Vital Perspectives and Practices for a Better World.
www.michelleholliday.com | www.thrivableworld.com

By Maria Ross

The Five Pillars of Effective Empathetic Leadership

"Efficiency is in. Is empathy out?" ran a provocative headline in the March 2023 issue of Fortune, implying that CEOs had to choose between people and performance, especially post-pandemic.

My work – and the research – say otherwise.

This false narrative forces us into a leadership paradigm that must choose between empathy or high performance, empathy or accountability, and even empathy or your own mental health. But the data and research clearly show that empathetic leaders and cultures boost a variety of performance vectors, such as engagement, retention, innovation, customer loyalty, inclusion, and customer satisfaction.

Empathy is a form of information gathering, where you put ego aside enough to listen to another point of view or understand someone's context so you can take a next right step together.

It is Not an Either/Or Paradigm. It is Both/And.

My work over the years has shifted from pure brand strategy, helping brands leverage empathy to better connect and engage with their ideal customers, to advising forward-thinking organizations how to leverage genuine empathy across their organization for stronger leaders, thriving cultures, and, yes, winning brands.

What is empathy at work? It is not crying on the floor with your employees. Empathy is being willing and able to see, understand, and (where appropriate) feel another person's perspective and to use that information to act compassionately.

Put simply, empathy is a form of information gathering, where you put ego aside enough to listen to another point of view or understand someone's context so you can take a next right step together. That step could be negotiating a compromise, giving them space, actively listening, laying people off with more compassion, upskilling an employee to succeed better in their role, or even counseling them out with full support and resources.

But many leaders are ill-equipped to practice empathy at work.

They falsely believe the common myths about empathy.

1. **They may believe it is a weakness.,** When it actually requires great strength to listen to another person's point of view without defensiveness or fear. And that doing so often leads to better business decisions, because diverse views can point out overlooked opportunities or risks.

2. **Or they believe empathy is about caving into unreasonable demands.** That is not empathy, that is submission. We can make tough business decisions but do so with empathy for those impacted.

3. **Finally, empathy is not about agreeing with someone.** We can listen to someone's point of view to understand better where they are coming from so we can perhaps choose a third path. We can now understand where they are coming from, even if we still do not agree. Empathy is about connection, not conversion.

The dark side of empathy is this: too many leaders, in the name of empathetic leadership, are sacrificing performance standards or burning themselves out trying to take care of everyone. They again have fallen victim to the false narratives of what empathy is and what it is not.

So how can leaders balance the needs of the business with the needs of their people – without burning out?

After years of research and hundreds of interviews, I deconstructed what made some leaders both empathetic and extremely high-performing. What made them the leaders people wanted to work for? Some of them did not even know why or how they did it until we delved into it.

I discovered five common traits and behaviours modelled by these empathetically healthy business leaders. Common threads that I saw over and over again.

The Five Pillars of Effective Empathetic Leadership.

When leaders are feeling burned out or that the team is not performing to their potential (or expectation), they may want to assess if any of these pillars need to be shored-up for themselves or their team culture.

Pillar 1: Self-awareness: To be empathetic, you must get your own house in order. Otherwise, you cannot take on other points of view without ego, fear, or insecurity. Emotional intelligence expert Daniel Goleman has

said, "If your emotional abilities aren't in hand, if you don't have self-awareness, if you are not able to manage your distressing emotions, if you can't have empathy and have effective relationships, then no matter how smart you are, you are not going to get very far."

Engage in self-assessment, reflection, and external feedback to better understand your own strengths, blind spots, leadership style, and emotional triggers. And help your team collectively understand themselves and how they interact. This can take the form of countless self-assessment tools like Enneagram, DISC, or Clifton Strengthsfinder, as well as peer and 360° reviews or working with a business coach, therapist, or trusted peer group. When you invest in helping people understand themselves better, you build a faster-moving, more innovative, and emotionally regulated workforce.

Pillar 2: Self-care: When your capacity is low, you have nothing left to offer others. Think about when you are tired or hungry; are you really able to be patient, clear-headed, or open-minded? Self-care goes beyond manicures and massages. It is not a luxury but a necessity. Self-care involves enforcing strong boundaries, taking

time to recharge your mind, body, and spirit in whatever ways work for you, delegating, resting, and stewarding one's own mental health as a leader. Empathetic benefits around self-care could include mental health days, unlimited paid time off, or employee assistance programs. When you are fully charged, you are better able to show up for your team – and you model this for your employees to keep them at optimal levels as well.

When you invest in helping people understand themselves better, you build a faster-moving, more innovative, and emotionally regulated workforce

Pillar 3: Clarity: Clarity is not just kind, it is empathetic. Resentments build where misunderstandings thrive. One of the biggest reasons leaders and workers clash is the lack of communication on mission, roles, and responsibilities. We cannot hold people accountable to an expectation we have not clearly set. Yes, empathy at work looks like clear career progression maps, clearly defined values (and what they look like in action), action-

able feedback, and discussing previously unsaid rules and norms of the team culture so no one is fumbling in the dark. In my work as a brand strategist, I have helped teams articulate their mission, vision, and values in useful and powerful ways that can be applied and measured to move work forward each day, not merely serving as a pretty poster on the wall.

Pillar 4: Decisiveness: Nothing is less empathetic than keeping people in limbo. Brain science shows us that a brain under stress or anxiety goes into fight or flight and does not fully engage critical executive functions, needed for innovating and problem-solving. Some leaders delay tough decisions or conversations in the name of empathy (*"I don't want to hurt their feelings"* or *"I want to find a decision everyone is happy with"*) but that is unfair to the team. Empathetic leaders who practice decisiveness do not merely dictate decisions – they encourage feedback and ideas but swiftly synthesize those inputs to make a firm call – and transparently explain why it was made that way. They address problems with curiosity and compassion before they fester, and they practice radical yet kind honesty.

Pillar 5: Joy: Yes, joy. Not that work is always fun, but creating a culture of levity, one where people can relax, build camaraderie, and friendships, and perhaps share a laugh goes a long way to enabling our brains to relax (see Pillar 4) so we can innovate and problem-solve. Even tough work environments such as ERs and police stations can create moments of levity that build trust and resilience. One C-suite leader cited his ability to laugh at himself and get to know employees personally made it easier to make big asks when times got tough. "They trust that I'm asking for a reason so they are willing to

Empathy means getting to know each other on a personal level, as human beings, to build trust and mutual respect

go the extra mile." The most empathetic and high-performing leaders also seek input from their team on how to create more levity and joy – they don't have to come up with all the ideas themselves.

You may notice that nowhere in these pillars do we advise "Being a total pushover" or "Never ask your team to work overtime". Empathy is more about mutual understanding and support than it is about acquiescence. In a work setting, it means getting to know each other on a personal level, as human beings, to build trust and mutual respect. It means ensuring everyone understands each other, their roles and goals, and the fundamental reasons they are being asked to perform specific tasks. The goal is not people-pleasing: it is to enable your teams to thrive and do their best work.

Without that understanding, it is easy to conflate compassion with concession.

It is vital to show leaders that we can leverage empathy to achieve radical success, but we have to be smart about it. We must take care of ourselves so we can continue the workplace and leadership paradigm shift that, quite frankly, was happening way before the

For too long, we have created leadership models that reward coldness, dictatorship, command and control.

Pandemic. The global crisis just accelerated the conversation faster than we could absorb it, for necessity's sake.

The balance between empathy and accountability can readily be achieved. We must embrace the Both/And paradigm so we can practice empathy without sacrificing productivity, profit, or purpose.

Empathy is a nuanced and complex concept that, unfortunately, many leaders get wrong. But if leaders can walk the tightrope, armed with the 5 Pillars, we will see our organizations flourish, our people live up to their potential, and the world at large benefit from the transformative impacts.

For too long, we have created leadership models that reward coldness, dictatorship, command and control. But our world has changed and to solve the complex challenges before us in the 21st century, we need leaders who can listen, recognize our common humanity, synthesize multiple perspectives, stay open to new ideas, and bring people together more quickly than ever.

Our leadership models are not laws of physics, We humans created these models, which means we can shift them.

Let's be crystal clear: the future of work is already here. We are living right now in the new era of work, and leaders are feeling the shift in challenging ways. Managers and leaders are being squeezed. They are being asked to take on a lot of roles: motivator, high-performer, doer, diversity champion, mentor, and driver of flawless results in a highly competitive landscape.

Leaders have three options to move forward:

They can revert back to the status quo and watch engagement plummet and their best talent walk out the door.

They can bend over backwards and grind themselves down trying to make everyone happy all the time. Spoiler alert: You cannot!

Or they can leverage the Five Pillars of Effective Empathetic Leadership and embrace empathy as a core value while simultaneously establishing boundaries, norms, and guideposts that protect leaders and team members alike.

I know which way I would choose. Do you?

Maria Ross *is a speaker, leadership trainer, empathy advocate and author of* The Empathy Dilemma *and podcast host of* The Empathy Edge. **www.red-slice.com**

By Kirstie Drummond Papworth

Self-Compassion

A Critical Resource for Leadership Success

Self-compassion is an indispensable leadership resource. Far from being a self-indulgent practice, it is a catalyst for resilience, emotional regulation, individual wellbeing and sustained leadership performance.

Compassion is a response to suffering, and it is important to acknowledge that everyone suffers – regardless of job title or status – albeit in different ways and at different times; a pressured, unsupportive working environment; a toxic boss; an overwhelming, undermining colleague; the daily juggle of responsibilities at home and at work. Redundancy, bereavement, illness. All of these are everyday examples of suffering, and no one is immune.

In simplest terms, self-compassion can be thought of as an awareness of our own suffering and a desire to alleviate such distress.

Writer and monk Jack Kornfield's statement, "If your compassion does not include yourself, it is incomplete" underscores the foundational role self-compassion plays in both professional and personal growth. While compassion for others is increasingly emphasised in leadership, self-compassion remains relatively under-utilized. This oversight is costly, as leaders who lack self-compassion are more prone to burnout, likely to be less effective in developing and sustaining healthy organizational cultures, and have limited resilience in the face of adversity.

This article examines self-compassion as a means of addressing our own suffering, its practical application in leadership, and its benefits for individual and organizational wellbeing. Drawing on both established frameworks and emerging research, I offer actionable insights for practically integrating self-compassion into everyday leadership practice.

Self-Compassion: Evidence and a Framework

Self-compassion is finally being acknowledged as a formidable means of enhancing psychological resilience, reducing stress and improving overall wellbeing. These outcomes therefore make self-compassion an appealing and useful leadership resource.

Recent research has repeatedly demonstrated the impact of self-compassion. Notable findings include brain imaging studies which reveal that self-compassion meditations activate areas associated with emotional regulation, such as the insula and amygdala. Another study, where participants simply imagined being the recipient of compassion, showed that these visualizations resulted in lower levels of cortisol, the primary stress hormone. In a rather wonderful experiment, Kaurin et al found that firefighters who had been exposed to significant trauma reported lower levels of depression when they practiced self-compassion. Repeated studies have found that compassion-focused interventions promote prosocial behaviours, which in turn help to improve team dynamics and cooperation at work, and can even reduce burnout in nursing staff.

As this increasing body of evidence illustrates, self-compassion is a powerful approach to dealing with stress, difficult emotions and even trauma. In order to benefit, it is useful to start by understanding what self-compassion actually is. In simplest terms, self-compassion can be thought of as an awareness of our own suffering and a desire to alleviate such distress.

The idea of practicing self-compassion might seem a little strange at first, particularly in a leadership context, and so a framework can prove useful. Psychologist and Professor Kristen Neff's widely accepted construct of self-compassion is comprised of three interconnected elements – mindfulness, common humanity, and self-kindness. I will now describe each of these in turn:

1.   *Mindfulness*

Although recent obsessions with mindfulness can be off-putting to many, Neff's definition is quite specific. In her approach, mindfulness involves acknowledging one's suffering without over-identifying with it or becoming

Self-kindness
'When I'm going through a very hard time, I give myself the caring and tenderness I need'

Mindfulness
'When something painful happens, I try to take a balanced view of how I feel'

Common Humanity
'When I'm down, I remind myself that there are lots of other people in the world feeling like I am'

overwhelmed. Such mindfulness allows leaders to stay present, observe their thoughts and emotions non-judge-mentally, and to avoid impulsive reactions that would be unhelpful in the workplace. This is therefore clearly a critical skill for any leader as they manage their way through challenge and complexity.

2. *Common Humanity*

This dimension reminds leaders that suffering is universal. Although in different ways and for a myriad of reasons, we all have moments of difficulty. Instead of

Mindfulness allows us to notice thoughts and feelings, without becoming overwhelmed by them.

asking "why me?" when things go wrong, this element encourages a recognition that "why not me?" might be a more useful question. This acceptance that no one entirely escapes suffering fosters a broader perspective and more regulated emotional balance. Understanding this shared nature of adversity can also support leaders to avoid feelings of isolation during difficult times, thus enhancing their capacity to cope during adversity and to empathize with their colleagues.

3. Self-Kindness

Self-kindness entails treating ourselves with the same gentleness and understanding that we might more typically extend to others. This practice can counterbalance tendencies toward excessive self-criticism, which can hinder decision-making and wellbeing. By practicing self-kindness, leaders model emotional intelligence and create a culture of psychological safety within their teams. This is often the aspect of self-compassion which people find most difficult, perhaps through lack of practice; if this is the case, think about what you might say to a friend or what they might say to you.

This framework is appealingly simple to understand and apply, yet self-compassion remains an oddity in leadership development. In a leadership context, self-compassion suffers from a reputational problem. In tough organizational life, it might be considered that such compassion for ourselves is a sign of weakness; those who cannot stand the heat should get out of the kitchen.

Self-compassion's Reputation Problem

Despite its well-documented benefits, self-compassion still faces resistance, especially in competitive corporate cultures where 'being tough' is often equated with competence. Prevailing cultural norms in many organizations often value self-reliance over introspection, creating stigma around practices perceived as 'soft'. Misconceptions equate self-compassion with vulnerability or indulgence, or just view it as unnecessary for some. Let's consider some of these concerns:

Self-Pity

Self-compassion can often be confused with self-pity. Sometimes, things just do not go our way, we have a run of bad luck or life can just feel like one long, hard slog. When we become preoccupied with such troubles and end up feeling sorry for ourselves, this is self-pity. Sometimes – and for a brief period of time – self-pity can be warranted, and without it we might miss gratitude and joy when life treats us more gently. But when we wallow in self-pity, we are largely viewing ourselves as victims of circumstances beyond our control. In psychologist Julian Rotter's terms, we would be exhibiting an external, rather than an internal, locus of control. Self-pity breeds passivity and excessive rumination, and leaders who remain stuck in such a state risk undermining their capability, credibility and emotional stability.

By way of contrast, self-compassion emphasises understanding and acceptance, resulting in better emotional regulation and resilience. Mindfulness allows us to notice thoughts of self-pity, without becoming over-

Self-compassion does not require an evaluation against others, and so our kind, considered focus can remain on ourselves rather than on the perceived flaws of others.

whelmed by them. Common humanity reminds us that everyone struggles and feels self-pity sometimes, and self-kindness encourages us to treat ourselves with the gentle kindness that we would offer a friend.

Self-Esteem

Some leaders may believe that improving their self-esteem reduces the need for self-compassion. Self-esteem refers to how we perceive our own worth or value, and this perception is often shaped by the opinions and actions of others throughout our lives. Our levels of self-esteem impact almost every aspect of our lives, from the quality of our relationships to our decision-making abilities and our overall sense of well-being. A moderate level of self-esteem can, of course, bolster our confidence and is correlated with positive wellbeing. However, if our self-esteem is too low then we are likely to suffer in terms of our mental health, relationships and resilience. At the other extreme, when self-esteem is too high, this can quickly lead to defensiveness and narcissism.

The main issue with self-esteem during times of difficulty is that when we are feeling low, accessing what we most like about ourselves is frustratingly difficult to do. In contrast, self-compassion is accessible even – nay, particularly – during periods of low self-worth and encourages intrinsic motivation for improvement. Leaders who practice self-compassion, rather than relying on self-esteem, can recover more quickly from setbacks, whilst also maintaining humility and inspiring trust.

Leaders who practice self-compassion avoid the paralysis of perfectionism or the urge to fight or flee fear, and so are better placed to evaluate options and take considered actions.

Self-esteem wants us to be better than average, and to achieve this we must therefore evaluate ourselves to be better than others. We must talk ourselves up while putting others down. More usefully, self-compassion does not require an evaluation against others, and so our kind, considered focus can remain on ourselves rather than on the perceived flaws of others.

Self-Criticism

Being our own toughest critic is worn as a badge of honour in some organizations, especially with those who might consider self-compassion as a weakness. In the words of fictional yet relatable CJ, boss of Reginald Perrin, "I didn't get where I am today by being nice". Of course, some self-criticism can be useful. It helps us to change behaviours or habits we dislike in ourselves and, when used in moderation, can assist us in assessing our achievements and actions. Excessive self-criticism, however, can be crippling, triggering stress responses and impairing mental health.

Where a growth mindset is prevalent, collaboration and innovation are more common, and employees report feeling more dedicated and empowered.

We often criticize ourselves more harshly than we would do others. Noticing such excessive self-criticism is a first step towards having a more compassionate attitude towards ourselves. Self-compassion mitigates the negative effects of self-criticism by fostering a more balanced perspective and reducing cortisol levels. Leaders who practice self-compassion avoid the paralysis of perfectionism or the urge to fight or flee fear, and so are better placed to evaluate options and take considered actions.

Being clear on what self-compassion is and noting how it is more useful than self-criticism, self-esteem or self-pity, offers leaders an opportunity to apply self-compassion with both understanding and clarity. Self-compassion is a powerful approach, offering leaders personal, professional and organizational benefits.

Benefits of Self-Compassion for Leaders

Many leaders remain unaware of self-compassion's tangible benefits, dismissing it as irrelevant to professional success, and even those with some awareness

may view self-compassion practices as low-priority, despite their long-term benefits. Particularly in a leadership context, there are numerous benefits of self-compassion, including emotional regulation, resilience after setbacks, a more innovative and collaborative mindset, and improved social relationships. Let us outline these in more detail, then offer practical ways to develop leadership self-compassion.

Self-compassion is a useful aid to emotional regulation. It enhances our ability to stabilize our moods, fosters optimism and reduces our susceptibility to stress. Simply put, leaders who practice self-compassion are better equipped to make thoughtful decisions under pressure. Emotional regulation generates trust, which also supports teams to navigate crises more effectively.

Resilience is the ability to recover from setbacks and is a vital skill for leaders navigating complex environments. This ability is critical in environments characterized by uncertainty and rapid change and, given the disproportionate impact of leadership, is an increasingly crucial leadership competency. Self-compassion enhances individual resilience levels by reducing rumination and enabling leaders to quickly bounce back from adversity.

The idea of a growth, as opposed to a fixed, mindset comes from psychologist Carol Dweck's work in this area. People who believe that their abilities and talents can be enhanced through their actions, smart strategies and feedback are said to have a growth mindset. Conversely, those who believe talent is fixed, even bestowed upon them, are considered to have a fixed mindset. The benefits of a growth mindset for individuals include better performance in tests versus of those with more fixed mindsets, increased intellectual abilities and more energy being allocated to learning. In organizations where a growth mindset is prevalent, collaboration and innovation are more common, and employees report feeling more dedicated and empowered. Leaders with growth mindsets inspire similar attitudes within

Compassion strengthens social connectedness, and the importance of this cannot be understated; poor social connectedness is worse for our physical health than obesity, heart disease and smoking.

their teams, driving innovation and collaboration. Juliana Breines and Serena Chen have shown in their research that practicing self-compassion can result in adoption of a growth mindset. This reinforces the importance of self-compassion for leaders; organizations led by such leaders are more agile and adaptive to market demands. Self-compassion, then, is good for leaders and for the results of the organizations they lead.

Practicing self-compassion has also been shown to bolster social relationships, promoting trust and cooperation, as well as fostering feelings of belongingness. These attributes are critical for leaders whose aim is to cultivate high-performing, cohesive teams. By showing appropriate vulnerability and self-compassion, leaders create inclusive, psychologically safe environments. It might sound fairly obvious to note that compassion strengthens social connectedness, but the importance of

Next time you make a mistake or do not live up to your own expectations, practice the three steps of self-compassion.

this cannot be understated; poor social connectedness is worse for our physical health than obesity, heart disease and smoking. Compassion, it seems, can even save our lives.

Practical Applications for Leadership

Addressing the reputational barriers and applying the insights from research requires a reframing of self-compassion as a critical, strategic leadership asset rather than a sign of fragility. Utilizing evidence-based techniques and integrating self-compassion into personal development practice can help leaders to develop and thrive, together with the colleagues and cultures they lead. This approach is closely aligned with Dalton's definition of leadership personal development as being the process of finding sustainable health and wellbeing.

Below are six practical ways in which leaders can start to develop their self-compassion; these are adapted from my book, *Compassionate Leadership for Individual and Organisational Change* (2023). It is worth bearing in mind that these are practices, so a consistency of approach will give better results than occasional grand gestures.

Practice self-compassion

Next time you make a mistake or do not live up to your own expectations, practice the three steps of self-compassion: Mindfully become aware of your feelings without becoming overwhelmed, remind yourself that everyone makes mistakes and suffers, and be as gentle on yourself as a good friend would be to you. Remember, through this practice, you will be improving your overall well-being and your leadership resilience.

Daily Self-Compassion Meditation

Through my own psychology research on the impact of self-compassion meditations on leaders, I found that listening daily to a short self-compassion meditation significantly reduced the participants' self-reported levels of stress, anxiety and depression. The practice of such meditations, even when as brief as three minutes long, can recalibrate leaders' stress responses and allow them to set a calm, focused tone for their day.

Adjusting Self-Talk

Leaders often engage in self-critical inner dialogue, particularly when things go wrong or if they consider self-criticism as having led to their successes to date. Reframing statements from overly critical "I'm a failure" to "I made a mistake, but I can learn from this"

Reframing statements from overly critical "I'm a failure" to "I made a mistake, but I can learn from this" transforms self-talk into a tool for growth and progress.

transforms self-talk into a tool for growth and progress. Reflective writing exercises can help identify patterns of self-criticism and develop more constructive alternatives.

Writing a Self-Compassion Letter

Acknowledging imperfections through writing oneself a compassionate missive can aid self-acceptance, even if it feels like a strange exercise at first. A self-compassion letter-writing exercise encourages leaders to treat themselves as they would a trusted colleague facing similar challenges. Start the letter by addressing it to yourself and bring to mind a difficult situation you would like to address; keep yourself safe in your choice of topic. Using the structure of the three aspects of self-compassion as a guide for three paragraphs can ensure you are practicing self-compassion rather than self-pity. If you choose to, it can also be useful to add a small action that you will take as a result of your contemplation about the specific scenario. Such self-compassion letters can also serve as enduring reminders of resilience and self-worth, and will often elicit surprising themes and emotions.

Leveraging Compassion Imagery

This technique effectively hacks our brain's inability to entirely distinguish between real and imagined. Being a recipient of compassion activates neural pathways associated with emotional soothing, and imagining a compassionate source soothing us reduces our stress responses. This simple technique, where we imagine receiving compassion for a few quiet minutes is shown to reduce anxiety and enhance our focus. Leaders can use such imagery techniques during high-pressure scenarios to enhance their confidence and clarity.

Creating a Self-Compassion Plan

Leaders can develop personalised self-compassion plans by identifying triggers of self-criticism and proactively applying techniques such as meditations, practicing self-compassion during difficult times and addressing repeating patterns of behaviour and emotion. Such plans allow for a deeply reflective approach to personal development, and serve as actionable roadmaps during high-stress periods.

Conclusion

By integrating self-compassion into their lives, leaders not only enhance their own wellbeing but also model healthy behaviours that benefit their colleagues and wider organizations.

The evidence is clear: self-compassion is beneficial to our wellbeing, resilience, relationships, leadership impact, and organizational results. Weaving self-compassion practices into our daily lives enables us to sustainably support ourselves, as well as to more effectively lead others.

A fully referenced version of this article is available on request from editor@dl-q.com

Kirstie Drummond Papworth *is a Psychologist and Executive Director at London Business School. She has Masters Degrees in Psychology and Behavioural Change, and is the author of 'Compassionate Leadership for Individual and Organisational Change', a finalist in the Business Book Awards and the Chartered Management Institute Book Awards.*

By Meena Kumar

Care is Cure

Beyond every role in an organization is a human mind and heart that is pulsing non-stop. Our 100,000-year-old brain is far behind in the evolutionary process and is grappling with digital realities. The core of human fabric is constantly challenged and compromises to this very fabric are turning real and frequent. Leaders at work constantly strive to match the speed of change while retaining their humane self, balancing emotional intelligence, care and compassion while leading. Conscious, emotionally intelligent workplaces are gaining attention in a ruthlessly competitive world. Organizational intricacies have seen context, content, data, and talent as frequently shifting pivots. Clearly, modern organizational life is very complex and stressful.

Many things have changed. I am unable to believe that innate human behaviours like care and compassion are now taught and are part of Leadership curricula. That is how complex we have become and how complex we have made the world. I come from a space where, as an HR Leader, you were expected to know every employee and understand her as a person beyond work. Today, I co-exist with a workforce in which chatbots respond to my queries and AI suggests best actions for me. This reality has left me baffled and I am adapting like most others to figure a way to co-exist with these inflections.

In hindsight, did I imagine an app that would remind me to breathe, drink water, walk, or monitor my heartbeat? Things that I thought were part of me are now beyond me and in some form, I feel a faint sense of external control over my core. I am in the middle of a techno-human evolution and forces from both ends beckon me. Multiply this view by millions of employees worldwide, the result can be astounding.

Humaneness will be the pivot for high-performing organizations, better societies and for holistic humanity. Workplaces that nudge for the best in empathetic relationships from employees and external partners are an act of art and science, and breed an ecosystem that is committed to holistic living and wellbeing

Alongside all of this, we are experiencing humanity and altruism in graded shades. The need for human connects has never been higher. Care and compassion are the new textures for a societal fabric and different textures evoke varied emotions.

Care is the new cure, the quest for Soulful workplaces is on.

Let us step back a bit.

What are a few turbulences and tensions that are keeping leaders awake and what are a few challenges that stare at us now?

1. **New inter-generational behaviours**: At work, we have a multi-generational workforce experiencing the human fabric differently. The multi-generational workforce is battling the real world of physical and emotional insecurities and threats. The world has pushed them to be in a constant "Flight or Fight" mode. Gen X saw stability and loyalty in the social fabric and care and compassion reigned supreme, while Gen Y and Z are facing huge shifts in the ecosystem of work and life. The need for acceptance is at an all-time high. Social media validation, pride in their video post going viral on the internet, mobile phones as a companion and anchor, tapping into information at the click of a button are behavioral

I am in the middle of a techno-human evolution and forces from both ends beckon me.

shifts that leaders are grappling with when it relates to the current generation. Acceptance, Acknowledgement and Recognition are constant asks from this generation.

2. **Shorter loyalty spans**: Leaders are also facing shorter loyalty spans. From a generation that joined and retired from a single organization to a generation that explored multiple organizations in their career span, to a gig workforce that is comfortable with short, skill-focused engagements, leaders are forced to accept these changes. The only constant through all of this has been the human continuity of care and compassion. The need for a dopamine – serotonin high through humane acts has been a constant.

3. **Narrowed attention spans**: The digital information overload and paradigm of endless choices have left the workplace with a fraction of attention span that must be shared between work, social media, and personal time.

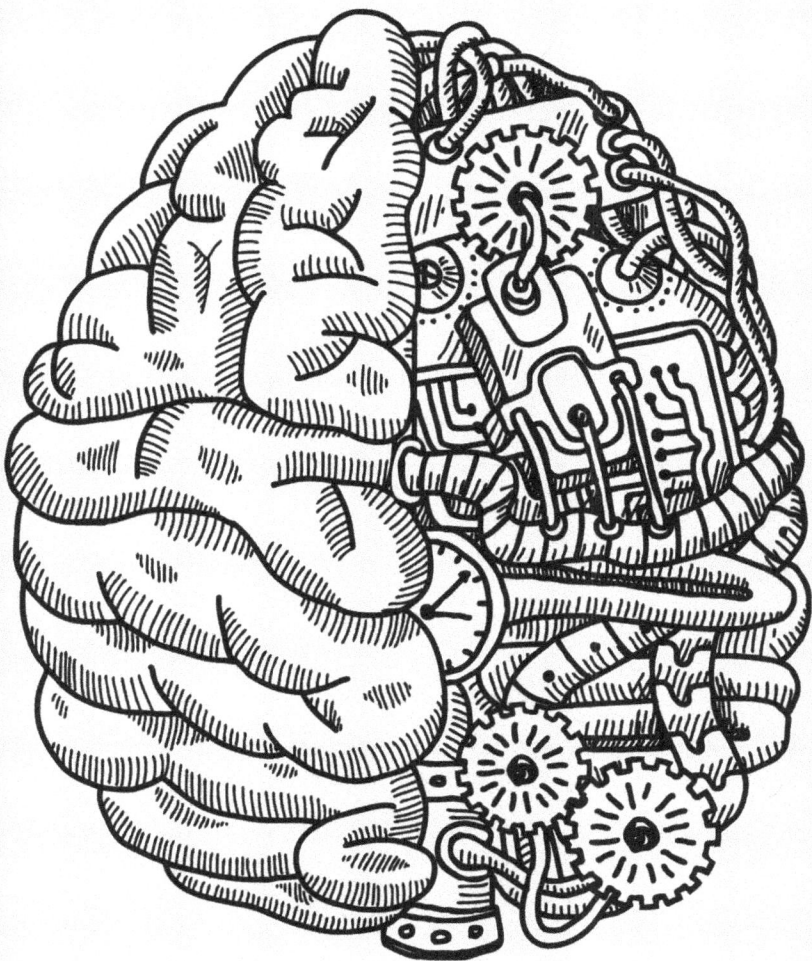

Our preparedness to listen deeply, empathetically, and listen to understand is a game changer for many workplace relationships.

4. **Conventional authority and hierarchy being questioned**: It is a common ask from the current workforce that a leader be more of a friend rather than be friendly at work

5. **Work life integration**: Being able to see career as part of life and not vice-versa.

6. **Other challenges** Networking opportunities, technology revolution, a demand for work-life integration, a sandwiched space for themselves with limited scope for expressing themselves fully, with ever evolving expectations from across the organization, and the mandate to adopt and adapt to changes are challenges that Leaders face.

7. **Evolutionary pace of teams**: Aspects such as right brain vs. left brain thinking in a fast-paced world; intellect vs. emotion at the workplace, speed of thought and ideation are sizeable evidence of a faster evolution of our workforce.

8. **An expansive Gen Z's desire for**: purpose, family time, sabbaticals, short-tenure skill-enriching jobs, fun@work, travel, and opportunities to satiate their materialism.

How should leaders engage with a workforce with varying needs, asks, learning and maturity curves?

1. **Hit the "Pause" button frequently**: To lead a multi-generational, demanding workforce who have moving goal posts and evolving expectations, the need for a leader to hit the "Pause" button to nurture her mind, emotions and soul mindfully is an imperative. Add in the element of empathy for the world around et voila!

   About a week ago, at lunch, a leader who had a difficult reputation, asked me how I maintained a calm and serene smile and added, "you have a graceful presence always". This is not new to me. Many people have complimented me for that. On reflection, I know it has not been an easy journey. It has taken me conscious effort to become who I am. Gracefully accepting situations, people and outcomes has chiselled and channelled my mind, heart and soul. Leading with logic, empathy and care has taken me years of practice.

   Listen with intent, and listen to understand: As leaders, how we engage with a spectrum of employees makes a mark. Our preparedness to listen deeply, empathetically, and listen to understand is a game changer for many workplace relationships. As leaders it is also about *how* we say things, not just *what* we say.

During a performance feedback conversation for a young, high potential employee, I had to convey the message that he needed to collaborate with the rest of the team. As I shared my feedback, his immediate response, in a slightly raised voice, was that he was delivering his work par excellence and had helped his team as needed. For a moment, I did not like his response, particularly the raised voice. I observed a fire on his face while he tried to battle his emotion underneath. I managed my emotion and used the tone of my voice assertively. It was gentle yet firm, I recall now. I stressed on collaboration however added, "Is there any way that I can be of help?" That was the game-changer. He instantly opened, shared all his piled-up challenges and let his emotions flow. I listened intently and realized that he needed acceptance from his team more than anything else. Taking this away, I spoke to the team in a different context and positioned him in the team positively. In a matter of weeks, the high potential employee briefed me about how excited he was to be part of the team and how much he enjoyed working there. Two powerful lessons that I learnt: What we see and hear need not always be true; there could be underlying emotions that can prevent people from being who they genuinely are. This incident emphasized the need for leaders to listen beyond the unsaid.

Unbiased lenses for people can better our ability in listening, empathy, and creating compassionate experiences for our teams.

2. **Don unbiased lenses:** When dealing with teams, try to create compassionate experiences that can go a long way in getting work done while wearing unbiased lenses. In a world where humanity is searching for an identity, there is not one person in the world seeking seclusion or solitude. Our world is a sum of every individual's primary and secondary socialization. This impacts the way each of us observe, integrate, and solidify our life narratives. We use this lens to filter people. Honestly, this one step can pull us back several fold while building positive, trusted relationships. Unbiased lenses for people can better our ability in listening, empathy, and creating compassionate experiences for our teams.

3. **Leaders must stay clear of self-doubt while leading.** Our experiences should not mask our ability to accept people the way they are. Our fleeting moments of angst, or anger should not mar our leadership sanity. The biggest question that is on most leaders' minds is "Who am I in this congregation of changes; am I good enough for the world of today?" Most indicated that they are at cross-

roads when they think about balancing the human fabric with the current social ecosystem. My conversations with several leaders over the years have left me curious. I am observing that leaders are increasingly leaning to Care and Compassion to touch a cord across employee populations.

Clearly, there is much work to be done continuously and consciously both by leaders and their teams. With the reality that we as humans will continue to retain Care, Compassion, Empathy, Intent, Humaneness, and Deep Listening even while change strikes us from everywhere, the least common multiple becomes the "Human Factor" in observing, assimilating, and interpreting workforce patterns at the workplace.

Leaders are increasingly leaning to Care and Compassion to touch a cord across employee populations.

A peek into the employee mind space

Today's employee is seeking answers. Constantly. Answers to questions like: What makes me happy? What keeps me happy? How do I stay happy? These are questions at work. Modern employees care for the past, the current and the future: purposed, purposeful, and purposable workplaces.

A natural extension then is, "How can employers create purpose-led workplaces while leading a purpose-driven employee base?

Why are we seeing this? The pandemic left the world with scars and wounds. It also provided ample time for families to re-unite, spend time with each other, make deeper connects, re-engage with their individual passion and purpose.

The Power of Care

Care is cure. Care is power. Care can foster a compassionate workplace. When care exists, there exists acknowledgement, support, understanding, wellbeing, positive interactions, and a positive workplace.

Care is now a Unique Selling Proposition and the new Employee Value Proposition too.

How can we build a Culture of Care and Compassion?

We cannot undermine the role and impact of Care, Compassion, Empathy and Emotional Intelligence in business: Customer-focus, Stakeholder-management, People-ecosystem, Leadership, Collaboration and Credibility. While technology will continue to be a pillar for revenue, speed and scale of work, the latent aspects of human relationships still emerge on top when it comes to conflict management, driving outcomes, or credibility building within and outside of organizations.

Leaders who dip into their reserve of human sentiments can take people along. The trusted bond and respect that leaders experience in being vulnerable is understated. Empathy and Trust as levers continue to drive organizational productivity.

While driving cultural transformation in organizations, as a leader my guidelines have been:

The latent aspects of human relationships still emerge on top when it comes to conflict management, driving outcomes, or credibility building within and outside of organizations.

- Be a role model for Listening and Compassion
- Steer with empathy while driving holistic wellness
- Recognize and appreciate teams: There is no better magic wand than the power of appreciation in nurturing a culture of care and compassion
- Seek opportunities to express gratitude for the efforts put in by teams.
- Create a respectful, and inclusive environment
- Push for managers to make time for their teams, the power of connect is unparalleled

What type of Leaders are admired in the current world context?

The modern employee is more driven by impact-creation, purpose, and balance than just maximizing income. Leaders with intent are cherished because the genuineness in them makes them stand apart. Leaders who

Workplaces that foster a sense of belonging, connectedness and camaraderie see high levels of employee engagement and people retention

thrive in a complex world with agility, with the ability to "Show Up" for teams, have the courage to accept that they do not know it all, have the heart and logic to provide growth and learning opportunities and Leaders who inculcate self-discipline to make time for personal and professional connects have a loyal following. Leaders with an ability to regulate their emotions, who are rooted, and balanced are most sought after in this chaotic world. Leaders enabling employee growth are admired. I have seen this repeatedly throughout my career across multiple organizations.

Why focus on care and compassion?

I believe that in an increasingly materialistic world, the old world charm of humanity still reigns tall. Humaneness helps in mental wellbeing, being able to go to bed with peace, that small moments of giving has shaped our career. Being humane is a serene and responsible feeling in an insanely competitive world.

Scientifically, data points to care and compassion as pillars to mental wellbeing and health. Altruism has paved the way for soulful workplaces. Workplaces that foster a sense of belonging, connectedness and camaraderie see high levels of employee engagement and people retention, the two people focus levers in every organization. A sense of being trusted and valued in the workplace also ensures employee tenure in an organization. When this is coupled with empathy and compassion, the results are manifold.

Soulful workplaces are engaging, motivating, and productive.

The human brain is receptive to leaders who care, are compassionate and who truly role model goodness without expectations. Employees who work with such leaders willingly stretch themselves to give their best, are eager to contribute and have their leader's back in challenging situations.

Creating a culture of care and compassion is a long term journey. It can start with baby steps, one day at a time, and can result in a grounded, purposeful workplace. The question that arises now is: How can we create a culture of Care and Compassion? Culture, simply put, is the way we do things. The way we do things stems from the way we behave, and the way we behave stems from the way we think. Working on our thinking process is the most complex element, yet becomes much simpler when we are able to form habits through rituals, tasks and consistent reminders to ourselves to do things in a certain way and to remember what to embed. Care and Compassion need reinforcements sadly in today's world.

Here are a few perspectives to consider while infusing Care and Compassion as levers to Leadership.

- Role model care and compassion in small steps, in every situation to ensure incremental impact on Culture;
- Communicate the impact of a compassionate and empathetic culture on Customer centricity, and how listening deeply and listening to understand creates wonders for customers;
- Socially, recognize leaders who display care and compassion consistently at work.

Soulful workplaces with care and compassion as peace forces are powerful at work. Such workplaces are engaging, motivating, and productive. Deliverables are delivered with a quiet sense of joy and altruism. While care and compassion are not the sole factors for career growth, they are two factors that can work favourably for us in difficult times. They act as invisible voices in our favour when we are not present in the room.

Workplaces and culture are evolutionary. Their evolution are incremental during ecological and emotional upheavals. The brain tries to hasten its attempt to adapt and we experienced this when COVID hit us. We were at our human best as we adapted to new ways of working while working through losses and being challenged with the ambiguity. This showed us the leadership mirror in more ways than one.

What are a few lessons I learnt as an outcome of the dynamics in the past few years?

- The human psyche stays strong irrespective of the turbulence around;
- Leading with a balance of the heart and intellect has a profound impact while driving results;
- Each leader has a unique DNA, and can impact through care, compassion and empathy

We are what Carl Sagan said "There is perhaps no better demonstration of the folly of human conceits than this distant image of our tiny world. To me, it underscores our responsibility to deal more kindly with one another, and to preserve and cherish the pale blue dot, the only home we've ever known". To which I add, "the earth's rotation has not accelerated, the sun and the moon have clarity in pace while we continue to run fastest to beat ourselves thin. Time to "Hit the Pause button" to slow down and manage the speed of life and its associated changes.

It will not be long until roles such as "Chief Care and Compassion Officer", Chief Happiness Analyst, Sabbatical Plan Experts will lead us to serene mental spaces. May care and compassion reinstate themselves and guide the human spirit in times to come.

Care is cure and is not esoteric anymore. What brought us here may not take us there! We need to shift from a mode of paranoia and panic to peace and purpose in the organizational context. Let us together attempt to create soulful workplaces and revive humanity at work.

Meenalochani Kumar (Meena) is a Neuroscience and Mindfulness Coach and a senior advisor at Sigmoid, the data science and analytics company. She has held senior positions with a number of multinational organizations, including Northern Trust Corporation and US IT-services company, Sutherland. Meena specializes in areas of Organizational Culture, Learning & Leadership, and Career architecture. Meena lives in Bengaluru, India. **meens72@ gmail.com**

By Judith Parke

Psychological Safety

Navigating Transformation in the Workplace

Introduction

n today's world, uncertainty is constant. From looming economic recessions to the escalating climate crisis, we find ourselves navigating uncharted waters. This uncertainty permeates every aspect of our lives and work, challenging our understanding of emerging technologies, future skill requirements, sustainable transitions, and the adequacy of our education systems.

At the organizational level, this macro uncertainty manifests in unprecedented changes across all sectors. We are witnessing a digital revolution powered by artificial intelligence and machine learning, evolving customer expectations, increased governance pressures,

Leadership promoting psychologically safer workplaces is essential for successfully navigating these turbulent times.

workforce transformations, and shifting generational demands. These changes are not mere adaptations or incremental improvements – they represent a metamorphosis akin to that of a caterpillar becoming a butterfly.

In this era of transformation, it becomes clear that leadership promoting psychologically safer workplaces is not just beneficial – it is essential for successfully navigating these turbulent times.

This is transformation, not change.

To take the UK energy sector as an example of the necessary shifts. There is huge pressure from government to increase national energy security following the war in Ukraine and rising conflict in the rest of the world. Ambitious targets have been set to ensure greener and more sustainable energy by 2035 including

- decarbonizing the electricity system,
- generating 66GW of offshore wind power,
- reducing reliance on natural gas.

Projections show a 50% annual increase in demand for electricity by 2035 driven by the

- increase in electric cars,
- electrification of industrial processes,
- installation of heat pumps as the leading source of domestic heating.

Costs are estimated at over £200 billion to achieve a renewable-powered economy, and challenges have already been identified with the existing network infrastructure; such as the ability to connect offshore wind farms, and battery technology that cannot yet smooth the variability of sustainable energy sources.

All this – and the transition needs to be just. It needs to meet targets for decarbonization whilst also preventing further fuel poverty; while managing job losses on the one hand whilst creating green jobs on the other; and also while we retrain and redeploy those whose roles are redundant, ensuring we do not leave the existing workforce and their communities behind as has happened in previous economic restructures.

Along with many other industries, the changes required to meet climate targets or avoid social inequity are under more scrutiny from interest groups and the wider public. Younger generations in particular are more demanding about the ethics of company operations.

This is just one example of one industry in one country, but this scale of transformation is happening everywhere.

Like any risk management, leaders and organizations have a responsibility to eliminate, mitigate or manage psychosocial risks.

In 2021, EY and the Saïd Business School at Oxford University formed a collaboration to study where transformation programmes go wrong. Their research suggests that 85% of organizations globally are either deep in the throes of transformation, or about to embark on the journey. Unfortunately, the data also tells us that most, up to 70%, of transformations fail.

The initial report, *The Future of Transformation is Human*, underlined just that. It is the human factors that influence whether or not transformations are successful.

Change is hard. Transformation harder.

There is inherent psychosocial risk in any change process. A psychosocial risk is the possibility of harm that can come from aspects of work such as work design (consistently high workload, lack of autonomy), interpersonal relationships (poor leadership or lack of psychological safety), poorly handled change management (micro-management, poor support), and negative work experiences such as verbal or physical abuse. Like any risk management, leaders and organizations have a responsibility to eliminate, mitigate or manage psychosocial risks.

Transformation processes by their nature carry heightened risk.

For example, change at this scale impacts all aspects of a business increasing uncertainty and job insecurity. This leads to heightened anxiety and stress among individuals and teams as people worry about the direct impact of decisions and changes. For those resistant to change, they are likely to disagree and disconnect with others whose perspective differs, leading to social isolation and relationship breakdown. This impacts team effectiveness, individual performance and everybody's mental health and wellbeing.

Internal communication is, therefore, key to any successful organizational initiative and never more so than in a transformation process. Anyone who has been through a significant change process recently knows that poor communication and a lack of clarity about process leads to rumours, mistrust, anxiety and, at worst, disengagement with the desired outcomes. All of which impacts performance, wellbeing and mental health.

Whilst some organizations can resource change, in others no additional resources are available. Transformation takes place alongside or on top of business as usual which can lead to overwhelm, excessive workloads and burnout.

Where ring-fenced resources for transformation are available, they regularly sit outside the day-to-day operations creating a disconnect. Those outside of the transformation team may feel their autonomy is eroded and a loss of control over the outcomes.

These are just a few of the predictable psychosocial risks.

In any workplace environment leaders need to create conditions to increase the likelihood of success. To do this, we need to understand the three basic environments team typically operate within and the role of the leader for each.

	Stable	Stressed	Distressed
	→	～⋀～→	🌀→
Conditions	· Predictable · Calm · High control	· Outcome uncertainty · High complexity · Limited control	· High pressure · Insecure · Low/no control
Example	**Business as Usual**	**Transformations**	**Sudden disruption**

Figure1 sets out the three environments team typically operate in, stable, stressed or distressed.

In stable or business as usual environments, leaders and teams have high predictability, expectations are clear, roles well defined and objectives agreed. Within a stable environment team harmony is key to working effectively. Effective leaders in stable environments are seeking to motivate their teams, giving autonomy, developing connectedness within the team and helping individuals seek opportunities for growth.

It is worth noting that for many people, the author included, a stable environment is a distant memory of a time before COVID-19, when offices where full, people travelled readily for work, and the level of disruption

For many people a stable environment is a distant memory of a time before COVID-19, when offices where full, people travelled readily for work, and the level of disruption faced was unimaginable.

faced and still being faced was unimaginable.

Distressed environments are caused by a disruption to business, either through a shock caused by external factors such as market crashes, environmental catastrophe or other unprecedented event such as COVID-19. Teams in distress have little or no control beyond responding to the immediate problems under intense pressure. The role of leaders in distressed environments is command-and-control, being a clear a visible authority as the team navigates the storm.

Distressed environments can also occur when ongoing stress tips over into distress. Transformation processes are by their nature long and arduous, some of the key risks highlighted above can create distress – poor leadership and communication, low autonomy, job insecurity – when managed badly.

The stressed environment may feel the most familiar to everybody just now. In stress, team are operating in high complexity, roles and responsibilities may be ambiguous and outcomes unclear. Due to the external forces driving transformation, leaders and teams can feel less in control of some of the factors determining decisions. The role of the leader here is to create psychological safety, both to manage effectively in the environment but also to lessen the likelihood of stress becoming distress.

Leading with psychological safety in stressed environments.

As *The Future of Transformation is Human* research identified, psychological safety is one of six conditions of human behaviour key to increasing a transformation's success nearly three-fold. The others are:

- purposeful vision
- adaptive leadership
- making it real with technology
- disciplined freedom
- and collaboration.

In her book *The Fearless Organization*, Professor Amy Edmonson defines psychological safety as the ability of any individual to speak up without fear of negative consequence. Asserting that in a knowledge economy the value of our people is what is in their heads, the capacity to problem-solve, collaborate, innovate and create. This is impossible if any individual feels their contribution would be negatively received or ignored.

Psychological safety fosters curiosity and an environment where individuals feel more able to take risks, and where people are more likely to embrace change. In teams with high psychological safety learning from failure is more common and individuals more likely to ask their colleagues for help. Psychological safety has also been shown to have an impact on employee retention.

For leaders, creating psychological safety means being able to model vulnerability and harnessing the power of 'I don't know'. Rather than creating more uncertainty, sharing vulnerability builds connection and trust

In teams with high psychological safety learning from failure is more common and individuals more likely to ask their colleagues for help.

with others. Leaders also need to invite participation, giving people opportunities to contribute and demonstrating that contributions are being listening to.

For psychological safety, trust is crucial, teams need to know they can trust their leaders and leaders need to know they can trust their teams and peers. In stressful environments, trust is more important than team harmony. This is two-fold, firstly we need to be clear not to confuse likeability with trust. We can all think of colleagues we would rely on to tackle complex problems at work, but we do not necessarily regard as a friend. This is a colleague we trust.

Secondly, leaders and their teams must be capable of engaging in constructive conflict. That is, able to discuss the big and difficult issues respectfully whilst maintaining interpersonal trust. In stressed environments, prioritising harmony leads to avoidance of difficult conversations, delaying decision making and erosion of interpersonal trust.

Three key tips for building psychological safety

- Provide a variety of channels and methods for feedback. Speaking up is often overweighted in terms of team contribution. It is important to recognise that some people prefer to contribute or feedback in writing, others need time to consider before inputting and in our current structures, those happiest to speak up and speak loudly are often given disproportionate credit.
- Psychological safety is not about being comfortable. Environments with high psychological safety will often be challenging, with people looking to learn and grow and able to have robust conversations.
- Building trust is fundamental. Creating a culture code where by all members of the team understand what is expected of them, their behaviours and responsibilities to others is a great way to establish a baseline of trust within a team.

In stressed environments, leaders who proactively build psychological safety are more likely to hear when things are at risk of tipping into distress, be able to engage their teams around short term period of intense delivery and or stress, and understand how to manage people through prolonged difficult processes.

A Wellbeing Roadmap for Successful Transformation

Intentionally
Prioritise
Wellbeing

Build your
leadership
capability

Create
psychological
safety

Respond to
distress safely

Track
performance

Consult a
Mental Health
Advisor for
guidance and
interventions

Any transformation process requires people to perform at their best and in the knowledge economy that means being cognitively fit.

Based on the research outlining the human factors required for a successful transformation, the knowledge the wellbeing is a pre-condition for high cognitive performance required for transformation, the understanding of the importance of psychological safety and our experience in developing effective systems to mitigate and manage distress within organisations, the Wellbeing Outfit have developed a Wellbeing Roadmap for a Successful transformation (see figure 1).

The roadmap has been designed to prepare, sustain and support people through transformation.

Intentionally prioritise wellbeing.

Any transformation process requires people to be optimized to perform at their best and in the knowledge economy, performing at our best means being cognitively fit. We need to help individuals understand and track what drives their wellbeing – eat well, sleep, well, exercise, engage non-work activity to maintain balance and destress – which helps both high performance and avoid burnout.

Tools such as

- wearable devices
- personalised wellbeing plans
- team Wellbeing Check-ins (sharing wellbeing priorities and being accountable to others)

can all help emphasise the importance of wellbeing and help individuals to prioritise their wellbeing.

Building Leadership Capacity

Do leaders have the skills and capability required for the change to come? For leaders to be effective they need to have confidence in their own leadership style while being adaptable to the environment around them. Leaders need to create clarity for teams with agreed roles, expectations and behaviours.

As the second phase of the EY research has shown, leaders' interventions at crucial moments can make or break transformations. Key to these interventions are leaders listening, sense making (understanding what is going on and how it is impacting people) and taking action. These three steps at key moments increase the likelihood of a significantly improved transformation performance by 12 times.

Leaders also need to stay the course; anecdotal evidence repeatedly highlights leaders leaning out as

change processes drag on. Many leaders are central to the decision making and further into the change curve than their team. To be effective, leaders need to lean into their teams throughout the change process, maintaining communication and connection.

Building psychological safety.

As outlined above, building psychological safety is key for leaders and their teams. Modelling vulnerability, prioritising trust over team harmony and even practicing constructive conflict within the team will help to build psychological safety. To practice constructive conflict, leaders can nominate roles to members of the team to ensure critical thinking, divergent views and opposition to the prevailing views are heard.

To be effective, leaders need to lean into their teams throughout the change process, maintaining communication and connection.

Respond Safely to Distress

Recognising these processes are inherently stressful and at points will be distressing to teams and individuals is vital. Organisations can mitigate against the risks and be better prepared to respond safely when distress inevitably occurs.

This means ensuring a large cohort of people across the organisation feel confident in spotting the signs of distress in others and understanding how to act. For example, training people to have supportive conversations and then signpost colleagues to help and support.

The organisation must have tools and partnership which can provide support appropriate to the situation. Responding to distress safely will help in the long term, minimising both the impact on the individual and the wider impact on the team.

Track Performance

Tracking performance is about creating measurements to provide indicators that can help leaders throughout the process, managing the known and unknown. From team resilience measures, collaboration scores, to pulse

Intentionally investing in the wellbeing and mental health of people at all levels is critical to success.

surveys; these data points provide opportunities for teams to feed in, and for leaders to step out of the weeds of the process.

Continuous measurement will also help leaders to assess the effectiveness of any interventions following turning points or pivotal moments where they have needed to intervene to keep the process on track.

Wellbeing/Mental Health Advisors

Having advisors and partners to work with who can help retain and manage the human factors in transformation is vital. Every business wants to move through transformation, retaining the best of their people and attracting new talent. Change management and transformation processes leave organizations radically different, but often wrung out, exhausted, with people slipping away, looking for other jobs, leaving because the process has been brutal, even if the outcome is what is required.

Intentionally investing in the wellbeing and mental health of people at all levels – leadership, those in the transformation team and everyone else in the organisation – whether they are staying or going in the long term is critical to success.

Conclusion

Transformation is an inescapable reality for most organizations today. It's a process full of inherent psychosocial risks that can significantly impact the well-being and performance of individuals at all levels. However, by intentionally prioritising the mental health and well-being of employees – from leadership to frontline workers – organisations can not only mitigate these risks but also enhance their chances of a successful transformation.

By placing humans at the centre of the transformation process, organisations can navigate change more effectively, retain their best talent, and emerge stronger on the other side. Remember, successful transformation isn't just about achieving business objectives – it's about doing so while preserving the health, well-being, and engagement of the people who make it all possible. In this era of constant change, creating psychologically safe workplaces isn't just a nice-to-have – it's a critical factor in determining whether an organisation will thrive or merely survive.

Judith Parke is UK Managing Director of The Wellbeing Outfit, and an associate director of the Scottish Leadership Institute. She has worked with major organizations in both non- and for-profit sectors across the world.

By Elana Friedman

Supporting Role Clarity Among Middle Managers

For the past few years, my colleagues and I have been working with an organization to explore how they develop leaders at different levels. We began with the executive team, helping them clarify their purpose as a team and the unique contribution they needed to make. This involved shifting their focus from leading *in* the organization—managing its operations and functions—to leading as leaders *of* the organization, setting its direction and holding its overall accountability. As we turned our attention to the organization's middle managers/leaders, a contrasting challenge emerged. While the executive team could clearly define their purpose and role, the middle managers/leaders struggled to do so.

Many in this group had risen through the organization, progressing from individual contributors to team members, and then to team managers/leaders. Promotions were often based on their technical expertise, but now, as middle managers/leaders, they found themselves navigating a complex space between management and leadership. We noticed that at times they referred to themselves or each other as middle managers and sometimes as middle leaders highlighted this complex role definition even further. Balancing these demands, understanding their unique contribution, and operating effectively in the "middle" was far from straightforward.

To address this challenge, we drew on a model developed by John Bazalgette and his colleagues at the Grubb Institute—the Transforming Experience Framework (TEF). Having worked with the model for a number of years with John and others at the Grubb Institute, I knew it as an invaluable tool for supporting clients in finding, making, and taking up their roles in organizations.

The TEF was developed through years of working with organizations and places the concept of role at its core. It is designed to help individuals gain clarity on their role and their unique contribution to their team or organization. What I find particularly valuable about this model is its integrated nature, orienting around both purpose and role. It sheds light on an area that is often opaque, offering a structured way to navigate this complexity.

At the heart of the model are three interconnected components—*person*, *system*, and *context*—which overlap at the central point of role. Together, they form a dynamic framework that highlights the factors influencing how we find, make and take-up our role and, crucially, *why* we take it up.

Understanding the TEF

Person

The first component, *person*, acknowledges that we bring our "person" to work. Our values, assumptions, desires, and life experiences shape how we engage in our roles. This is an essential insight because it draws attention to the mindset we carry into the workplace. Edgar Schein's iceberg model illustrates this well, showing how much of what influences our behaviour— our assumptions and values—sits "below the waterline," unseen but powerful.

In organizations, we often hear opposing ideas: "leave yourself at the door" versus "bring your full self to work." The TEF offers a middle ground. It recognizes that while we bring ourselves—our values and beliefs,

In organizations, we often hear opposing ideas: "leave yourself at the door" versus "bring your full self to work." The TEF offers a middle ground

assumptions, skills, and experiences—to work, how we choose to show up is also influenced by the other two components: *system* and *context*.

System

The second component, *system*, refers to the social systems we are part of. For many, our first experience of social systems often comes from family or community, where we learn to navigate spoken and unspoken rules. Organizations are another form of social system, with their own cultural norms, values, and behaviours. Within these larger systems, there are often multiple subsystems, such as departments, teams, or hierarchical levels, each with unique cultures and expectations.

For middle managers, this complexity is particularly pronounced. They frequently straddle multiple systems, each with its own boundaries and norms. A key part of the TEF is developing an awareness of which system you are operating in at any given moment and understanding its boundaries. This can be especially fluid for middle managers, who must navigate between roles such as managing up, leading their teams, and collaborating with peers.

Middle managers frequently move between systems, shifting hats as leaders, managers, or collaborators

Context

The third component, *context*, refers to the external factors shaping the system. For instance, a sales department in a financial services company operates within the broader context of the financial industry, shaped by regulations, market trends, and competitive pressures. These contextual factors influence the system's demands and, in turn, how an individual takes up their role within it.

Bringing It Together

The TEF brings these three components—*person, system,* and *context*—together to offer a nuanced understanding of role. It acknowledges the interplay between our personal values and experiences, the systems we are part of, and the external context influencing them.

But the model goes further. It doesn't just explore *how* we take up our role; it also addresses *why*. The TEF emphasizes that our role is ultimately in service of the system's purpose. What this means, is that as we consider our role we need to orientate ourselves to the purpose of the a particular system we are in. This focus on purpose makes the framework particularly valuable for middle managers.

For middle managers, clarity on purpose is often harder to achieve than for executives. While executive teams typically operate within a well-defined system, middle managers frequently move between systems, shifting hats as leaders, managers, or collaborators. To take up their roles effectively, they must continually ask: Which system am I representing in this moment? What is the purpose of this system? Without this clarity, it becomes difficult to orient their role and navigate the complexities of the middle space.

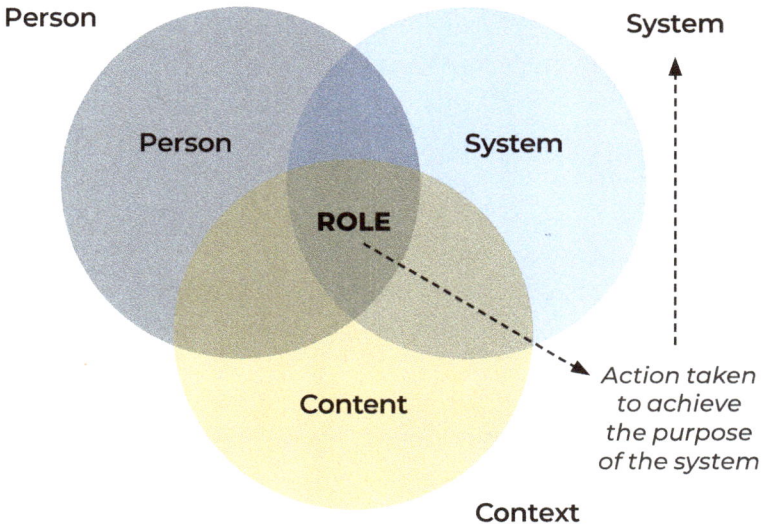

Action taken to achieve the purpose of the system

Middle Managers often act as the linchpin between executive priorities and the needs of teams who deliver on those priorities.

Applying TEF to Middle Managers

Middle Managers often act as the linchpin between executive priorities and the needs of teams and staff who deliver on those priorities. This asks of middle leaders to navigate the needs of executives, their teams, and peers putting an additional pressure for role clarity and understanding of which purpose they are working to. The TEF helps them to navigate these complexities in the following ways.

The "Person" Component: Self-Awareness in Role Clarity

The person component of the TEF reminds us that middle managers bring their values, assumptions, and past experiences into their work. These personal factors shape their approach to leadership and decision-making. However, the demands of middle management require balancing these personal drivers with the expectations of others. Role clarity, enhanced through self-reflection

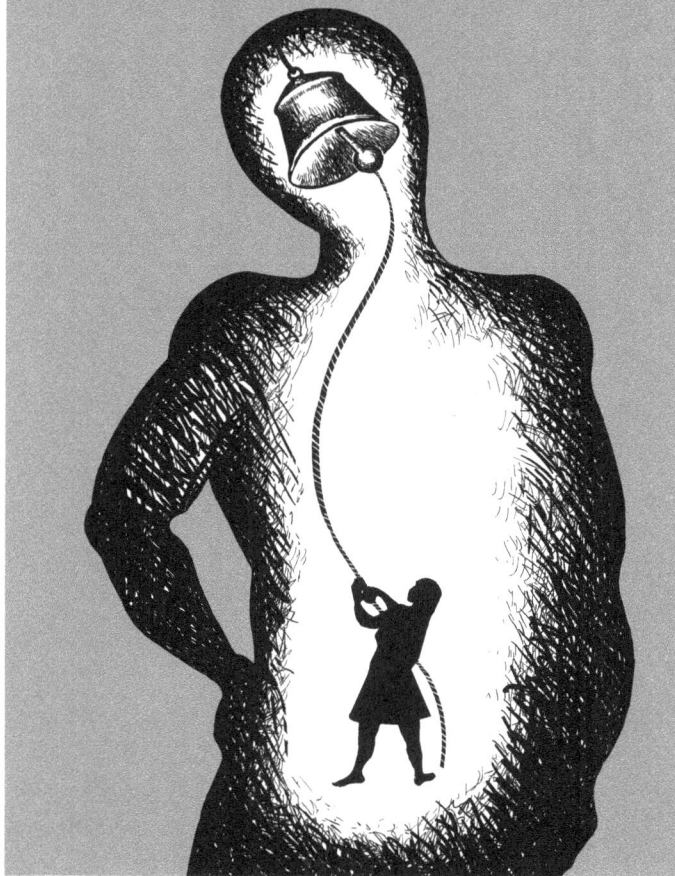

and feedback, helps managers manage this balance effectively. The TEF encourages middle managers to surface these influences and consciously align them with organizational goals. As leaders of others, it also stresses the importance of being aware of what motivates others, what their values and assumptions are. Knowing this

The system component acknowledges that middle managers operate within complex organizational ecosystems.

enables the middle manager to build relationships, understand what motivates team members and what culture will enable their teams to thrive. Understanding the person is also key to supporting their staff to build resilience and enhance their well-being.

The "System" Component: Navigating Social Systems

The system component acknowledges that middle managers operate within complex organizational ecosystems. These include not only the overarching company culture but also the subcultures of teams, departments, and levels. Middle managers must navigate these systems while managing relationships both upwards and downwards.

TEF provides a way to map these systems, understand their boundaries, and identify the cultural norms at play, enabling managers to adapt their behaviour to fit different contexts. With the clear focus on system purpose, it also forces middle managers to seek out and clarify what the purpose of the system is, a question that is often left unexplored. It encourages middle managers to have the right conversations with the right people to create alignment and clarity on what purpose they are working to. This also helps to support their leadership of others and enables others to get clarity of their role in service of the system purpose.

The "Context" Component: Responding to External and Internal Drivers

Finally, the TEF emphasizes the importance of understanding the external drivers and their impact on the systems in which managers operate. By developing systemic thinking and aligning their actions with contextual demands, middle managers can better bridge the gap between strategic priorities and operational realities. Bringing in the component of context also encourages middle managers to look up and out, to see the bigger picture and understand the interdependencies within the organization.

In practice, the TEF offers middle managers a roadmap and a way of understanding and clarifying their role. When I work with clients, we often apply it in the following ways:

- **Map the systems** – Take time to map the various systems that they interact with daily and identify what the key purpose is of each of these systems. Also take time to understand the cultural norms within the systems. For example, we worked with a group of middle managers in a healthcare organization to map the systems they navigated daily. Within their own team, their focus was on meeting departmental targets, such as driving sales and revenue. When collaborating with other middle managers across the organization, their role shifted to aligning market insights with the organization's broader purpose of maximizing customer satisfaction. In community health meetings, they represented the organization, prioritizing collaboration and relationship-building. Seeing the various systems and the purpose of those systems, enabled the middle managers to find, make and take up their role with clarity.

- **Engage in team and organizational conversations** – having taken time to map the systems and identify the purpose of the systems, we encourage middle managers to engage in team and organizational conversations to ensure clarity and alignment of purpose and role. This helps to create connection of expectations across the organizational hierarchy and within and across teams.

- **Looking in and looking out** – in mapping the various systems, we then encourage middle managers to notice what falls into the context, both from within the organization and further outside the organization.

This focus on context, means that middle managers are lifting their eyes up and out to see what lies beyond the boundary of the system they are in. For example, when the middle managers are sitting in the departmental system, the organizational purpose and priorities or industrial standards fall into the context. This is a reminder to look beyond their own departmental boundaries when setting work tasks to keep in mind the wider context.

- **Enrol those around you** – role clarity is not just an individual responsibility but also a system/ organizational one. Enrolling other leaders in this way of thinking strengthens team cohesion and organizational effectiveness.

- **Cultivating a reflective practice** – take time to reflect on what is influencing your leadership and management. What values are driving your behaviour? Assumptions are key drivers to how we behave. Bringing reflection to notice and name your own and others assumptions is key. The more we are able to become aware of which assumptions we need to challenge as they no longer serve us, or hold lighter. By this we mean not to hold onto them so tightly as "truths", but give space for the possibility of their being another assumption that can be more helpful to hold. The more aware you are of what is driving your own

practice, and the more curious you can get of what is driving others practice, the more you can step into your leadership with intention and awareness.

Extending the Purpose of Role Clarity

In our experience, the organizations that are most effective and focused are those where the organizational purpose is explicitly and continually linked to role purpose. This means that employees at all levels understand not only what their role is required to deliver, but also why it matters within the broader organizational mission. For instance, the classic story of the cleaner at

The classic story of the cleaner at NASA who saw their role as "helping to put a man on the moon" illustrates the power of creating a clear "line of sight" between role and organizational purpose

NASA who saw their role as "helping to put a man on the moon" illustrates the power of creating a clear "line of sight" between role and organizational purpose.

To take this alignment to the next level, organizations need to articulate not just what a role must achieve but how the role should be performed. In doing this attention is brought not only to the task and output, but the relationship or dynamic and outcome the organization is seeking from the individual. This requires defining, by role and by level:

- **What good outcomes look like:** Clarity on the tangible deliverables and results expected from the role.
- **What good leadership behaviour looks like:** Clear descriptions of the behaviours and values that support those outcomes.

In our experience, this clarity can be rigorously reinforced through mechanisms such as performance management, talent development, and even remuneration strategies. For example, we worked with an orga-

High performance is about 'what' you deliver, and also 'how' you deliver.

nization, where individuals are annually appraised not only on what they deliver but also on how they behave as leaders, managers and team members.

This approach encourages individuals to evidence their performance, fostering both accountability and reflection. It shines the light on the idea that "high performance" is about what you deliver, along with how you deliver. This also encourages a different kind of conversation and culture in the organization. It asks of managers to have the challenging conversations (or what we call the essential conversations) that face into questions of behaviour, engagement with others and the manner in which you take up your role in the organization. We have noticed that organizations that have this built into their appraisal system and lean into these essential conversations tend to have healthier cultures. All of this helps to foster and reinforces the importance of purpose-driven management and leadership.

As organizations continue to navigate complexity and change, middle managers remain vital to bridging strategy and execution and leading on embedding purpose-led role clarity. By embracing frameworks like the TEF, they can gain clarity and confidence in their roles, which in turn strengthens their ability to lead effectively across the multiple systems and contexts they encounter. This clarity enables them to act with greater intentionality, aligning their contributions with the organization's purpose while supporting their teams to do the same.

Moreover, as middle managers cultivate this understanding, they foster stronger connections within and across teams, building resilience and cohesion that ripple throughout the organization. Their ability to map and navigate systems, understand contextual drivers, and engage in purposeful leadership becomes a catalyst for organizational agility and sustained success.

The question that remains is this: how can organizations ensure that middle managers are not just supported but empowered to find, make, and take up their roles fully? By embedding frameworks like the TEF into leadership development strategies, organizations can create environments where middle managers thrive, driving not only their own growth but also the broader mission and purpose of the organization.

Elana Friedman *(elana@middle-ground.co.uk),founder of MiDDLEGROUND, is a dynamic and experienced individual and team coach. Her clients highlight her ability to foster purposeful conversations that tackle immediate issues and the underpinning systems and beliefs that need to shift. Elana has worked across Africa, Asia, Central America, the UK and Europe.*

By Samir Selmanović

The Immigrants' Journey

Learning to Lead Others Where You Have Never Been Before

"He who travels gently, travels safely; and he who travels safely, travels far."
Joseph Thompson, Scots Explorer in 19th Century

n his 1949 tome, *The Hero with a Thousand Faces*, Joseph Campbell synthesized his massively influential mythic model of the 'Hero's Journey'. Even if you don't know it by name, you know it in substance. From the Mesopotamian epic of Gilgamesh, written around 2100 BC through Homer's Iliad to Star Wars, Harry Potter, and almost every Hollywood movie, the Hero's Journey format endures in how we narrate our lives and decipher our leadership challenges.

The Hero's Journey format endures in how we narrate our lives and decipher our leadership challenges. Yet human experience also gives rise to different stories.

The vast majority of stories in the West are one version or another of the Hero's Journey. Campbell, somewhat obliviously, labels it and praises it as a monomyth. The Hero's Journey has incredible explanatory power of our experiences. Yet, human experiences can give rise to different explanations and stories. At the moment, we are in danger of finding ourselves on the depleted soil of a monomyth. (*Discover more about the strengths and drawbacks of the Hero's Journey in this related article on the DLQ digital pages: **tinyurl.com/beyond-heros-journey**)*

Over the years, this has led me to imagine what could be another kind of journey and story conflict that we need now—one that is more accurate about our present condition and more generative for our times.

I have been experimenting with the concept of the Immigrants' Journey in leadership development contexts with delightful results. It goes like this: We are immigrating into the future.

Stuck Heroes

When my daughter Leta was on her hero's journey in the dragon land of her high school, at the very same time, I was on my hero's journey of slaying my dragon. I was to become a New York City teenage daughter's parent. She, trapped in thinking this story was all about her dealing with the challenges of clueless parents and the magical yet treacherous world of her high school, and I, trapped in thinking this story was all about me dealing with the crowning mid-life task of protecting and passing on the wisdom to my posterity. Two stuck heroes.

I thought, what if I cease seeing this as *my* journey? So, I told her, 'We have never had this sort of relationship before. I don't know what I'm doing. You don't know what you are doing. Let's help each other immigrate into territory that's new for both of us.'

I told her, 'Look, we are entering this world where I'm learning to be a teenager's parent, and you're learning to be an adult. It's new for you. It's new for me. I feel lost. You feel lost. What if there's no need for this push and pull to see whether you can deal with me or I can deal with you? Let's invite ourselves to immigrate to a new place where we both dare to experience being different. It would be a step into a new land where both you and I would be displaced together. Do you want to do this?'

In contrast to roadmapping or GPSing, which detach us from the landscape, wayfinding is a skill of leading as we go.

Every story needs a conflict, and we had a better conflict. Instead of heroes needing villains and victims, the challenge was in us discovering and entering a new way of seeing, doing, and relating.

We crossed the threshold into the unknown. The heaviness lifted, and fresh air enveloped us. This was quite a different story. Mobilizing, sturdy, dangerous, joyful. It was exciting! The new perspective affected my parenting from then on and fundamentally changed us. Today, we are still leading and following each other.

We took the Immigrants' Journey. Notice the plural pronoun.

I now approach my life, love, and leadership differently. I adjust how I see who we are and who we are becoming. With heroes, villains, and victims in cameo roles, I found myself in a place of far more possibilities. I started using this concept in my executive coaching, consulting, and speaking. There were stuck heroes everywhere I turned.

Another Kind of Journey

In contrast to the Hero's Journey, the Immigrants' Journey is not sequential or neat. It resembles life more closely. We are all invited to live lives greater than we can control and lead others to learn to do the same. So, there are no Campbell's 17 steps that fall in place. There are no stages. Anything can happen at any time, anywhere and we find stability in our common human capacity to respond to life in real time, re-interpret our past, and have grounded faith in the future. We do not roadmap. We wayfind.

Wayfinding is an irreducibly human capacity to live, love, or lead through uncertainty. It confronts us with the astonishing fact of being here now, insists on giving meaning to our experience, and meets our needs for belonging and becoming. In contrast to roadmapping or GPSing, which detach us from the landscape, wayfinding is a skill of leading as we go. There is always a new way emerging.

Wayfinding, the earliest human capacity to move from known to unknown, has been well-researched by anthropology and neuroscience. Every species has its umwelt (one of those nifty German words) directly translated as "world-around." It conveys the uniqueness of the species' genius. We humans have this one thing that separates us from every other species: Left to ourselves, we walk into the unknown, befriend it, and learn to delight in it. We can't help it. It took us a mere 20,000 years from grunting about our plan to catch dinner together to developing the theories about the universe's consciousness. We are wayfinders.

Immigrant is a contemporary and more recognizable word for wayfinder. We continuously find a new home, take on new responsibilities, and become someone new.

Wayfinding has been our way since time immemorial. The very first human power was to find ourselves curious or frightened enough to get out of the confines

Immigrant is a contemporary and more recognizable word for wayfinder. We continuously find a new home, take on new responsibilities, and become someone new.

of our shelters. Then we walked to the end of the familiar territory, then forward and forward again, learning to survive and thrive by finding a way we have never been on before. Walking, talking, inventing fire, wheel, mirror, juicing, soccer, and computing came as we went about our real business of befriending the unknown.

The true gift of wayfinding is not the arrival at the destination. It is who we become along the way. It is not that we have been finding a way out there; it is that we have changed as we did. Our wayfinding is as inner as it is outer. Yes, our world's problems seem insurmountable. We know we cannot simply do what we have done in the past. But we are not doomed. Here is the good news: we are not the same humans we were back then and can do something we have never done before.

One more thing. In more personal terms, wayfinding is also about learning your particular way of traveling toward your horizon. Whenever we cross a critical threshold, we enter the unknown realm and temporar-

Knowing how to travel well may be the best definition of happiness. And to help others learn to do the same, the most rewarding view of leadership.

ily disorientate. We become inner-life wayfinders as we discover the creativity that can only come with the experience of being a bit lost.

Immigrating is about knowing how to take your next very ordinary step, and then next, and then next, alone and in company, always learning, always looking back to the pliable past and forward with our hearts tethered to the horizon that is calling. Knowing how to travel well may be the best definition of happiness. And to help others learn to do the same, the most rewarding view of leadership.

There is one non-negotiable quality of a leader: Having faith in the future. You have to believe that the unknown will not only serve new dangers and challenges but also supply you with new energy, truth, and joy. None of us have any business leading without this sort of faith in ourselves, others, and the world. As Michael Margolis, the leading authority on narratives for disruption, puts it, "Disruption sucks. So, give people faith in the future."

You, an Immigrant

Before we go on, a clarification.

We think of immigrants as other people. Those of us who have been in a stable geographical configuration are not used to thinking of ourselves as immigrants. But we are. We *all* are.

We are all displaced. Whether or not someone is from this company, community, or country does not matter. Everything around us is shifting. It is not that we have moved into a different place; it is that a different place has surrounded us. Look back. We are not where we were a year ago or even a month ago. Transition upon transition upon transition. It is bewildering. In the new world of informational, political, and scientific ,overwhelm' and escalating complexity, none of us feel at home as we used to.

We are all on the move from the known into the unknown—everybody. There is no home for the hero to return to. We are creating new homes as we go, and it is as scary as it is exhilarating. It is not that we are vulnerable. It is that we are vulnerable together. "It may be argued that the past is a country from which we have all emigrated, that its loss is a part of our common humanity," says Salman Rushdie.

Leaders with whom I have shared this invitation to see themselves as immigrants felt empowered, particu-

We are all displaced. Everything around us is shifting. It is not that we have moved into a different place; it is that a different place has surrounded us.

Perspective is today's leader's defining asset—not more information, not more time, and not more power.

larly if they were not geographical immigrants. "Now I know why I feel the way I feel. I am an immigrant too," they would say. "This helps me lead others with more empathy and imagination."

Three Skills that Matter

Let's select and review three immigrant skills that can make our leadership more robust.

1. Perspective

It is entirely possible to change one's perspective.

Nobody knows this better than immigrants. Almost by definition, *only* immigrants know the meaning of having a new perspective.

As we immigrate, we change not only the answers to our questions but also the questions themselves. With the new questions, we change where our attention goes. And where our attention goes, our mind and heart have opportunity to follow.

If our perspective can change, everything can change. Without embracing our status as immigrants, we fully invest ourselves in defending and perfecting our established views, which is another way of safeguarding the biases that have been running our lives in the known that is no more.

Immigrants, on the other hand, are willing to drop their old maps for a moment. They have to. As mathematician Ludwig Wittgenstein put it, "The limits of language are the limits of my world." Instead of looking for a villain, immigrants focus on learning a new language. Made of new words, concepts, or experiences, this language can be literal, nonverbal, emotional, cultural, business, or a new kind we don't even know yet.

Immigration can occur from country to country, from system to system, from this to the next epoch of our lives. In each case, it is a journey from one way of seeing to an additional way of seeing everything. Two ways of seeing are far more than double. It is experiential proof, a bodily experience and the memory of that experience, that there is truth, kindness, and beauty outside of the way we are used to being in the world. That is a mystical moment.

Perspective is today's leader's defining asset—not more information, not more time, and not more power. When the tsunami of information, knowledge, and wisdom is drowning us, people follow the leaders who will help them get on a hill for a better perspective.

How do you see?

That is what matters. Your perspective determines how you show up in every moment and what stories you tell.

2. Practice

It is entirely possible to change one's practice.

Immigrants embrace the role of apprentice again. Instead of observing change and talking about it, chasing an illusion of managing change, or indulging in calling themselves change agents, they learn to inhabit change.

This is humbling. Rainer Maria Rilke writes in a poem, "The purpose of life is to be defeated by greater and greater things." Immigrants acknowledge the forces larger than their own lives and are finding their way to survive and thrive in a story larger than their own.

We live and lead in a reality far larger than what we can control. Yet, there is one thing we can control: our practice. While navigating the new landscape, our previous views become difficult to maintain. Our new experiences no longer fit our old explanations. Our practice adds new experiences, and new experiences make new and more useful explanations possible.

We are entering a new landscape with old maps, gravitating to answers based on the intuition that has sustained us in the past. Our intuition is our capacity to have a lucid moment that helps us deal with complexity.

You will not become who you wish or strain to be. You will become who you practice becoming.

However, it is based on our experiences up to the present moment. That is why we have to recalibrate our intuitions with new experiences. Without updating them as we go, our intuitions deteriorate into biases.

On a more personal level, we can never control the outcomes the way we can control what we do day-to-day, the rituals, the habits, and others routines.

The artists stand with one foot in the known and one in the unknown, communicating from that place to us. They do not have control of their communication's impact, but they do have control of their process and practice. A painter cannot paint six masterpieces at will, but she can create her masterful practice of showing up in the shop and doing her thing her way six hours a day. The results are not up to her, but the process is.

This is the case with the change artists, too, which is another name for leaders.

Controlling results is daunting personally, professionally, and spiritually because it is impossible. Even if it were possible, control would render our lives deathly dull. We live in a complex system made of complex systems. But complexity does not have to be complicated. It is possible and critical to respond to complexity overload with some form of radical simplicity. More likely than not, such radical simplicity will be in the form of practice.

A thought leader on how to live in complex times, Jennifer Garvey Berger asks a helpful question we can use: "Who have I been, and who am I becoming?" I think this less of a question of pondering and more of a question of observing. You will not become who you wish or strain to be. You will become who you practice becoming.

What is your practice of becoming?

We want our life and leadership to produce something of great value, and here is the kicker: The practice is that something. In economics-speak, the practice is the product.

3. Participation

It is entirely possible to change how we relate to the world.

We begin our adult journey when we finally cross the threshold called 'I'm enough'. Once we utter this with conviction, it is a joyful new beginning with a wide-open floodgate of confidence and accomplishments. That is what lots of leadership coaching for people in their 20s, 30s, and even 40s is about. Later in a leadership career, the path of growth leads through realizing something quite startling: Actually, I am not enough.

Everything that matters to us, lasting and meaningful, cannot be done alone. In some ways, our early career resistance to saying 'I am enough' is a premonition of the future discovery that, in some fundamental way, 'I am' in fact, not enough. As Carl Jung puts it, 'The first half of life is devoted to forming a healthy ego, the second half is going inward and letting go of it.'

Hero's epiphany: I am enough. Immigrant's epiphany: I am not enough. Both are necessary. This is one of the reasons we cannot afford to live with a monomyth.

What is it that you want but can never accomplish

When the time is right, cross the threshold called 'I'm not enough.' Then, ask for help and offer help.

alone? Go and give your best to that, and you will soon realize that your best is not enough. You merely (and gloriously!) participate.

When the time is right, cross the threshold called 'I'm not enough.' Then, ask for help and offer help. This is one of the most crucial thresholds one has to cross on the way to executive-level leadership. Your participation is not what you do when you cannot do leaderly things. Your participation is the highest calling and experience of leadership.

Being an immigrant never resolves. You continually take the risk of trusting the unsafe world. Which is the only way we can walk into the future.

I play the role of leader as needed. Others play the role of leader as needed. We all participate. The story is largely not about me. It is like the meaning of Ubuntu: 'I am what I am because of who we all are.'

The Invitation

Leadership at its best is modelling followership. A leader is a lover. We love and care for something deeply, so much so that we are willing to get lost in order to find it.

The unknown is dangerous. It is also a place where our not-yet-known collaborators, questions, and answers await to be found. It is all so exciting!

We are willing to enter the borderland where we continually leave and arrive. It is not a phase. It is a place where we are learning to make our home now.

We live more than our own heroic story. We discover other stories, participate, and sing our songs, old and new, perhaps all night long, like immigrants do.

The unknown is dangerous. It is also a place where our not-yet-known collaborators, questions, and answers await to be found. It is all so exciting!

Unlike the Hero's Journey, the Immigrants' Journey is not a story of defending our perceptions until the strife teaches us otherwise. We are not blinded to the ordinary mysticism of being where we already are. Instead of bending others to fit our story, we invite them to our story and let them invite us to theirs.

Often, we don't need or even want to be heroes. With all its dangers, the unknown is also waiting for us in friendship. We don't know who we will become but are not frightened because whoever we become will catch us.

Leaders who learn to articulate a new way of journeying to their people in a plausible, felt, and pragmatic way will touch them the way the Hero's Journey used to touch people, eliciting a nod of recognition and giving expression to a new and newly alive language that can meet the challenges we face.

Let's summarize our three leadership tips:

1. Perspective: Watch over the way you see.
2. Practice: Do what is yours to do.
3. Participation: Enjoy leading *and* being led.

Leadership is an invitation. Whether to our daughters, organizations, teams, board members, friends, or enemies, we say, "Let's not go where I am, as beautiful as that place seems to me. Let's not go where you are, as wonderful as that place seems to you. Let's go together to a place that neither you nor I have been before."

Samir Selmanović, *Ph.D., helps leaders stop trying too hard and meet complex challenges with radical simplicity, skill, and joy. He's coached 500+ leaders and helped 20+ organizations transform themselves, drawing on his expertise as an engineer, pastor, and psychologist. www.samirselmanovic.com*

By Hamilton Mann

Artificial Integrity Over Intelligence Is The New AI Frontier

As AI systems increasingly take on critical roles across healthcare, education, transportation, finance, and public safety, relying solely on computational power and intelligence without embedding integrity into their design represents a major flaw.

On the path to advancing AI with integrity over intelligence, five critical characteristics—yet current limitations—come to mind as priority concerns.

Safety: While AI can quickly process data, it does not inherently consider whether its actions are safe, legal, or

While AI can quickly process data, it does not inherently consider whether its actions are safe, legal, or ethical.

ethical. An illustration of this is the near-perfect execution of imitating a person's identity traits and characteristics, made possible by certain systems, without any verification, prevention, or restriction. This can lead to what we call deepfakes and severe consequences affecting individuals' reputations, privacy, or safety, and also lead to broader societal harms such as misinformation, manipulation in politics, and fraud.

Fairness: Some AI systems have taken steps to reduce harmful biases in their responses by training them on diverse datasets and continuously fine-tuning them to avoid producing unethical outputs. However, this is still an ongoing challenge. Even among the best image generation applications powered by GenAI, biases persist, such as when these tools suggest image modifications that reflect stereotypical or sexist cultural clichés, which can offend certain populations and perpetuate discriminatory biases.

Values: We can assume that an AI system that we use in our daily life has been designed to align with broadly accepted values and cultural settings. However, as its value system is shaped by its training data, it does not necessarily reflect cultural ethical norms.

It does not "learn" values, culture and social norms dynamically after deployment in the way a system with integrity might. It may be updated periodically by its developers to improve its alignment with values, but it does not adapt autonomously to changing contexts. It lacks the autonomous reinforcement learning system where it could continuously learn and improve its behavior without human intervention.

The rush towards AI is no excuse for irresponsibility.

Explainability: While some AI systems can explain certain processes or decisions, many AI systems cannot fully explain the decision-generating process (i.e., how they generate specific responses). Those based on Machine Learning, and even more so, those based on more complex models like deep learning are often opaque to users and operate as "black boxes." While these systems may produce accurate results, users, those affected by the systems, and even developers often cannot fully explain how specific decisions or predictions are made. This lack of transparency can lead to several critical issues, particularly when they are used in sensitive areas such as healthcare, criminal justice, or finance.

Reliability: Some GenAI systems, such as ChatGPT, are designed to provide useful information, but true artificial integrity would involve a higher degree of consistency in ensuring that all information provided is reliable, verifiable with sources, and fully respects copyright of any kind, so as not to infringe on anyone's intellectual property. AI with embedded integrity would analyze the data it processes and produce results that adhere to all relevant copyright laws, ensuring respect for creators and protecting against legal challenges.

All of these essential characteristics are related to a specific trait, which is not intelligence but integrity.

Without integrity embedded at its core, the risks and externalities posed by unchecked machine intelligence make them unsustainable, and render society even more vulnerable, even though they also bring positive aspects that coexist.

The excitement and rush towards AI is no excuse or tolerance for irresponsibility; it is quite the opposite.

The responsibility is to shift towards ensuring that AI systems operate with integrity over intelligence—safeguarding human values, and upholding societal imperatives over raw intelligence.

The question is not how intelligent AI can become, whether it involves calls for super artificial intelligence or artificial general intelligence. No amount of intelligence can replace integrity.

The question is how we can ensure AI exhibits Artificial Integrity—a built-in capacity to function with integrity, aligned with human values, and guided by principles that prioritize safety, fairness, values, explainability, culture and reliability, ensuring that its outputs and outcomes are integrity-led first, and intelligent second.

The difference between intelligent-led and integrity-led machines is simple.

What Artificial Integrity systems are

The difference between intelligent-led and integrity-led machines is simple: the former are designed because we could, while the latter are designed because we should.

Without the capability to exhibit a form of integrity, AI would become a force whose the impact of evolution is inversely proportional to its necessary adherence to values and its crucial regard for human agency and well-being.

Just as it is not sheer engine power that grants autonomy to a car, nor to a plane, so it is not the mere increase of artificial intelligence that will guide the progress of AI.

This perspective highlights the need of AI systems to function considering the balance between "Human Value Added" and "AI Value Added" where the synergy between human and technology redefines the core design of our society, while preserving societal integrity.

Systems designed with this purpose will embody Artificial Integrity, emphasizing AI's alignment with human-centered values.

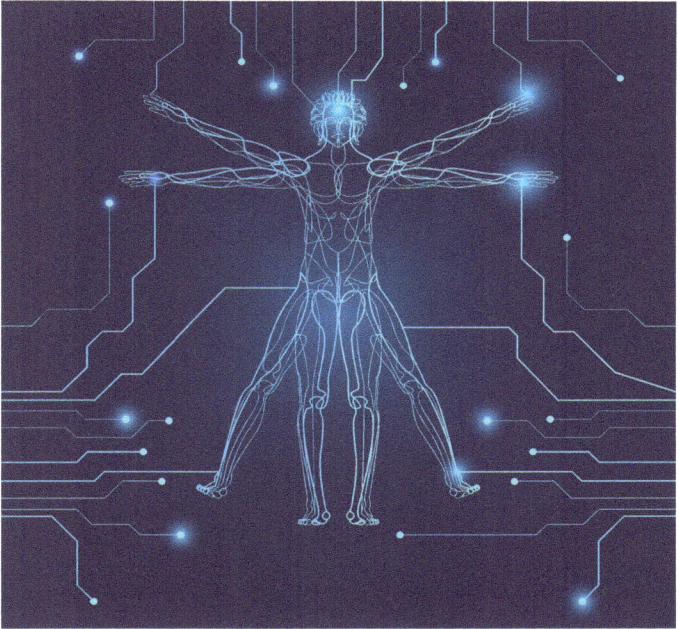

A world predicated on Artificial Integrity would look vastly different from today, primarily because AI systems would be designed to prioritize not just intelligence and efficiency, but value models that ingrain, by design, the requirements of explainability, fairness, values, safety, and reliability in particular.

To systematically address the challenges of Artificial Integrity, organizations can adopt a framework I defined, structured around three pillars: the *Society Values Model*, the *AI Core Model*, and the *Human and AI Co-Intelligence Model*.

The Society Values Model revolves around the core values and integrity-led standards that an AI system is expected to uphold.

Each of these pillars reinforces each other and focuses on different aspects of integrity, from AI conception to real-world application.

The *Society Values Model* revolves around the core values and integrity-led standards that an AI system is expected to uphold. This model demands that organizations start to consider doing the following:

- Clearly define integrity principles that align with human rights, societal values, and sector-specific regulations to ensure that the AI's operation is always responsible, fair, and sustainable.

- Consider broader societal impacts, such as energy consumption and environmental sustainability, ensuring that AI systems are designed to operate efficiently and with minimal environmental footprint, while still maintaining integrity-led standards.

- Embed these values into AI design by incorporating integrity principles into the AI's objectives and decision-making logic, ensuring that the system reflects and upholds these values in all its operations while

optimizing its behaviour in prioritizing value alignment over performance.

- Integrate autonomous auditing and self-monitoring
mechanisms directly into the AI system, enabling
real-time evaluation against integrity-led standards
and automated generation of transparent reports
that stakeholders can access to assess compliance,
integrity, and sustainability.

This is about building the *"Outer"* perspective of
the AI systems.

The *AI Core Model* addresses the design of built-in
mechanisms that ensure safety, explicability, and transparency, upholding the accountability of the systems and
improving their ability to safeguard against misuse over
time. Key components may include:

- Implementing robust data governance frameworks
that not only ensure data quality but also actively mitigate biases and ensure fairness across all training
and operational phases of the AI system.

- Designing explainable and interpretable AI models
that allow stakeholders, both technical and non-tech-
nical, to understand the AI's decision-making process,
increasing trust and transparency.

- Establishing built-in safety mechanisms that actively
prevent harmful use or misuse, such as the genera-

tion of unsafe content, unethical decisions, or bias amplification. These mechanisms should operate autonomously, detecting potential risks and blocking harmful outputs in real time.

- Creating adaptive learning frameworks where the AI is regularly retrained and updated to accommodate new data, address emerging integrity concerns, and continuously correct any biases or errors with regard to the value model that may occur over time.

This is about building the *"Inner"* perspective of the AI systems.

The *Human and AI Co-Intelligence Model* emphasizes the symbiotic relationship between humans and AI, highlighting the need of AI systems to function considering the balance between "Human Value Added" and "AI Value Added", where the synergy between human and technology redefines the core design of our society, while preserving societal integrity.

They would be able to function considering four distinct operating modes:

Marginal Mode: In the context of Artificial Integrity, *Marginal Mode* refers to situations where neither human input nor AI involvement adds meaningful value. These are tasks or processes that have become obsolete, overly routine, or inefficient to the point where they no longer contribute positively to an organization's or society's goals. In this mode, the priority is not about using AI to enhance human capabilities, but about identifying areas where both human and AI involvement has become useless.

One of the key roles of Artificial Integrity in *Marginal Mode* is the proactive detection of signals indicating when a process or task no longer contributes to the organization. For example, if a customer support system's workload drastically decreases due to automation or improved self-service options, AI could recognize the diminishing need for human involvement in that area,

AI systems need to ensure explainability, by showing how they arrive at their conclusions.

helping the organization to take action to prepare the workforce for more value-driven work.

AI-First Mode: Here, AI's strength in processing vast amounts of data with speed and accuracy takes precedence to the human contribution. Artificial Integrity would ensure that, even in these AI-dominated processes, integrity-led standards like fairness and cultural context are embedded.

When Artificial Integrity prevails, an AI system that analyzes patient data to identify health trends would be able to explain how it arrives at its conclusions (e.g., a recommendation for early cancer screening), ensuring transparency. The system would also be designed to avoid bias—for example, by ensuring that the model considers diverse populations, ensuring that conclusions drawn from predominantly one demographic group don't lead to biased or unreliable medical advice.

Human-First Mode: This mode prioritizes human cognitive and emotional intelligence, with AI serving in a supportive role to assist human decision-making. Artificial Integrity ensures that AI systems here are designed to complement human judgment without overriding it, protecting humans from any form of interference with the healthy functioning of their cognition, such as avoiding influences that exploit vulnerabilities in our brain's reward system, which can lead to addiction.

In legal settings, AI can assist judges by analyzing previous case law, but should not replace a judge's moral and ethical reasoning. The AI system would need to ensure explainability, by showing how it arrived at its conclusions while adhering to cultural context and values that apply differently across regions or legal systems, while ensuring that human agency is not compromised regarding the decisions being made.

Fusion Mode: This is the mode where Artificial Integrity involves a synergy between human intelligence and AI capabilities, combining the best of both worlds.

In autonomous vehicles operating in *Fusion Mode*, AI would manage a vehicle's operations, such as speed, navigation, and obstacle avoidance, while human oversight, potentially through emerging technologies like brain-computer interfaces (BCIs) would offer real-time input on complex ethical dilemmas. For instance, in unavoidable crash situations, a BCI could enable direct communication between the human brain and AI, allowing ethical decision-making to occur in real time, blending AI's precision with human moral reasoning. These

kinds of advanced integrations between human and machine will require Artificial Integrity at its highest level of maturity. Artificial Integrity would ensure not only technical excellence but also ethical, moral, and social soundness, guarding against the potential exploitation or manipulation of neural data and prioritizing the preservation of human safety, autonomy, and agency.

Finally, Artificial Integrity systems would be able to perform in each mode, while transitioning from one mode to another, depending on the situation, the need, and the context in which they operate.

Considering the *Marginal Mode* (where limited AI contribution and human intelligence is required—think of it as "less is more"), *AI-First Mode* (where AI takes precedence over human intelligence), *Human-First Mode* (where human intelligence takes precedence over AI), and *Fusion Mode* (where a synergy between human intelligence and AI is required), the model *Human and AI Co-Intelligence* ensures that:

In crash situations, a BCI could enable direct communication between the human brain and AI.

- Human oversight remains central in all critical decision-making processes, with AI serving to complement human intelligence rather than replace it, especially in areas where ethical judgment and accountability are paramount.
- AI usage promotes responsible and integrity-driven behaviour, ensuring that its deployment is aligned with both organizational and societal values, fostering an environment where AI systems contribute positively without causing harm.
- AI usage establishes continuous feedback loops between human insights and AI learning, where these inform each other's development. Human feedback enhances AI's integrity-driven intelligence, while AI's data-driven insights help refine human decision-making, leading to mutual improvement in performance and integrity-led outcomes.
- AI systems are able to perform in each mode, while transitioning from one mode to another, depending on the situation, the need, and the context in which they operate.

Reinforced by the cohesive functioning of the two previous models, the *Human and AI Co-Intelligence Model* reflects the *"Inter"* relations, dependencies, mediation, and connectedness between humans and AI systems.

This is the aim of Artificial Integrity.

Systems designed with this purpose will embody Artificial Integrity, emphasizing AI's alignment with human-centered values.

This necessitates a holistic approach to AI development and deployment, considering not just AI's capabilities but its impact on human and societal values. It is about building AI systems that are not only intelligent but also understand the broader implications of their actions.

An essential element in building such an Artificial Integrity model lies in the data process.

Beyond labeling, which generally refers to the process of identifying and assigning a predefined category to a piece of data, it is necessary to adopt the practice of annotating datasets in a systematic manner. While labeling data gives it a form of identification so that the system can recognize it, annotating allows for the addition of more detailed and extensive information than simple labeling. Data annotation gives the data a form of abstract meaning so that the system can somehow contextualize the information.

Including annotations that characterize an integrity code, reflecting values, integral judgments regarding these values, principles underlying them, or outcomes to be considered inappropriate relative to a given value model, is a promising approach to train AI not only to be intelligent but also capable of producing results guided by integrity to a given value model. For example, in a dataset used to train an AI customer service chatbot, annotations could include evaluations on integrity with respect to the value model referenced, ensuring that the chatbot's responses will be based on politeness, respect, and fairness. Training data could also include annotations about ethical decision-making in critical scenarios, or ensure data is used ethically, respecting privacy and consent.

Another essential element for an AI model capable of displaying features of artificial integrity lies in the training methods. AI trained using supervised learning techniques that allow the model to learn not only to perform a task but also to recognize integrity-led and preferred outcomes is a promising path for the development of artificial integrity. It is also conceivable to add information about the value model used to train a given AI model through data annotations and then use supervised learning to help the AI model understand what does and does not fit the value model. For example, regarding AI models

*Data annotation gives the data
a form of abstract meaning
so that the system can
contextualize the information.*

that can be used to create deepfakes, the ability to help the system understand that certain uses indicate deep faking and do not match the value models would demonstrate artificial integrity.

Another complementary approach is to design systems where human feedback is integrated directly into the AI model learning process through reinforcement learning methods. This could involve humans reviewing and adjusting the AI's decisions, effectively training the AI model on more nuanced aspects of human values that are difficult to capture with data and annotations alone. Especially when it comes to global AI models, thus used in many countries around the world, users across these different countries should have the opportunity to express their feedback on whether the model aligns with their values so the AI system can continue to learn how to adapt to the different value models they impact.

Building AI systems with Artificial Integrity presents several challenges that must be carefully addressed to ensure they operate ethically and responsibly. One major difficulty is the subjectivity of values—different cultures, communities, and individuals may have varying perspectives on what constitutes ethical behaviour.

Moreover, scalability poses another challenge. Annotating large datasets with detailed integrity codes requires significant resources, both in terms of time and human expertise, and may not always be feasible in practice. This process can be further complicated by the risk of bias introduction—the annotators themselves may unintentionally embed their own biases into the AI system, leading to skewed or discriminatory outcomes.

To overcome these issues, it is critical that AI systems are designed with mechanisms for continuous learning and adaptation. AI models equipped with Artificial Integrity must evolve alongside shifting ethical standards and societal values, which can be achieved through ongoing human feedback loops and dynamic updates to the annotated data. This could allow the system to recalibrate its decisions as cultural contexts or ethical norms change over time.

One of the most pressing design challenges of our time

Artificial Integrity is unattainable by AI developers working in isolation—ethicists, sociologists, public policy-makers, domain experts, diverse user groups and more must be involved from the outset to ensure a comprehensive approach that reflects a range of perspectives. This collaborative effort is essential for creating AI systems that are not only technically advanced but also grounded in a well-rounded, integrity-driven foundation.

Overall, this is a subject that requires more researchers to build AI that upholds human values over the pursuit of performance for the sake of performance.

As Warren Buffet said, 'In looking for people to hire, look for three qualities: integrity, intelligence, and energy. And if they don't have the first, the other two will kill you.'

This principle equally applies to AI systems.

How to prevent such systems to be used to generate propaganda or manipulate public opinion on a large scale, as this could destabilize political and social systems even more than we see today?

How to protect people from becoming overly reliant on AI for critical thinking and decision-making as this can result in diminished human judgment and expertise in areas like education, law, and even healthcare, where the value of human intuition, empathy, and ethical reasoning are critical (if not irreplaceable)?

How to ensure the training process of AI does not lead to unintended privacy violations, particularly when AI systems begin to interact with sensitive data at scale?

How to mitigate AI environmental costs such as increased water consumption, CO_2 emissions, rare earth mineral extraction for hardware production and the exacerbation of e-waste?

These are some of the questions that need to guide AI model design, prioritizing Artificial Integrity over Intelligence, which therefore aligns with the societal model we envision for the future.

Hamilton Mann is Group Vice President of Digital at Thales, AI for good pioneer, author of Artificial Integrity, senior lecturer at INSEAD and HEC Paris, mentor at MIT's Priscilla King Gray Center. He was inducted into the Thinkers50 Radar.

By Orit Wolf

Leadership Lessons through Performers' Hands

n a disruptive era marked by extensive interdisciplinary collaboration, exploring insights from various fields to enhance leadership practices has become crucial. This article presents practical tools and fresh perspectives drawn from musicians and performing artists aimed at enriching leadership practices for scholars, executives, and organizations seeking to expand their strategic approaches. At the Technion, Israel's leading university for science and engineering, a new workshop titled "Leaving Your Mark in Science & Arts" has been developed for MBA professionals and those in interdisciplinary studies. Taught by Dr.

Cultivate a leadership mindset that emphasizes listening, agility, and creativity, enhancing overall leadership capabilities.

Orit Wolf, an international concert pianist, lecturer on personal impact and leadership, and *Artist in Residence*, the course offers participants innovative exercises that integrate artistic principles with performing arts examples. The course aims to cultivate a leadership mindset that emphasizes listening, agility, and creativity, enhancing overall leadership capabilities. By exploring concepts such as the Art of Conducting as a non-verbal activity, Ensemble Rehearsing, Reverse Engineering of Success, and the Role of Improvisation, this course equips scholars and business leaders with a nuanced understanding of leadership, drawing from impactful practices in the performing arts.

A. Conducting – Leadership Lessons through Non-Verbal Communication

Much research has been conducted on leadership and non-verbal communication in general, as well as on conducting styles and leadership. To provide students with a more personal and impactful experience, they were given a digital questionnaire to complete while watching video recordings of four renowned conductors: Leonard

Bernstein, Herbert von Karajan, Richard Strauss, and Gustavo Dudamel. The questionnaire asked participants to observe various components in each conducting style, such as facial expressions, hand movements, body movements, use of a baton or no baton, and eye contact. The primary assumption was that students, even if they were not musicians, could easily observe these elements and identify the leadership style of each conductor and how he mentored his players through non-verbal communication. Participants received a multiple-choice questionnaire to choose from five different leadership types: Autocratic, Bureaucratic, Democratic, Charismatic, and Transformational leadership. They were then asked to share which conductor they would prefer to work with if they were active performers. The results were striking, ranging from initial hesitation to definitive opinions. Each participant felt they could easily trace both the non-verbal communication methods and the leadership style of each conductor, and they clearly stated who they would like to perform under, all within the brief experience of watching each conductor for less than five minutes.

An additional exercise involved watching the same symphony, Beethoven's Symphony No. 5, conducted by different conductors. This reinforced the validity and impact of non-verbal communication between a conductor and their players. The distinct interpretations of the symphony showcased how the same musical piece could sound different under each conductor's direction. Pasher and Porat (2020) emphasize that the conductor's unique role is to provide a tone while allowing each player a chance to shine and evolve with the rest. This balance, according to them, is what creates a successful harmonic orchestra (Pasher et al., 2020).

Another fascinating example comes from Bobby McFerrin's methods of rehearsing. As a conductor, singer, entrepreneur, and inspirational lecturer, McFerrin created a disruptive rehearsal with the Israeli Philharmonic that exemplifies creative leadership. In that video, McFerrin has the players sing their parts instead of playing their instruments. Although it may initially seem absurd for musicians to sing Rossini's Overture of The Barber of Seville instead of playing, this exercise highlights disruptive leadership. By having the orchestra members sing, McFerrin allows them to be "equal" to one another, as every player uses the same instrument—their voice. This removes the hierarchy of traditional roles, enabling the players to connect through eye contact and experience real teamwork. They not only enjoy the surprising musical result but also engage in a genuine sense of solidarity and collaboration.

This seemingly simple exercise offers valuable leadership lessons. It demonstrates that the impact of leader-

> **The primary assumption was that students could easily identify the leadership style of each conductor through non-verbal communication.**

ship is not about having significant facilities but about the creativity and approach of a leader who engages with the orchestra in a memorable and disruptive manner. McFerrin's method illustrates how shared leadership values and creative approaches can leave a lasting impression.

Leadership Case Study in Action

An exercise from the MBA course "Leaving Your Mark" at the Technion mirrored the insights gained from observing conductors. In this exercise, students were paired and assigned a negotiation topic to debate, progressing through three distinct stages:

Stage 1: Each pair engaged in a verbal argument while seated across from one another, utilizing full hand movements to emphasize their points.

Stage 2: Participants argued with their hands positioned behind their chairs, thereby removing the use of body language.

Stage 3: In this stage, each pair invited another pair to join them. The new pair's task was to sit behind the original speakers and mimic appropriate hand gestures, synchronized with the ongoing argument. The original pair, seated in front, continued their verbal exchange without using their hands, while the second pair silently conveyed the corresponding gestures. This setup created a unique dynamic where one pair focused solely on verbal communication, and the other emphasized non-verbal cues, highlighting the powerful role of body language in enhancing or diminishing the clarity and persuasiveness of an argument.

This exercise parallels the conductor's role, akin to Bobby McFerrin's innovative methods. Just as McFerrin uses unconventional techniques to foster cohesion and creativity in his orchestra, the exercise highlighted how leaders must effectively use non-verbal cues to enhance

Orpheus employs a rotating team leadership structure, fostering shared influence and collaborative creativity.

their influence and communication. By understanding and leveraging non-verbal communication, leaders can create more impactful and resonant interactions, much like a conductor shaping a memorable performance.

B. Cultivating Constructive Teamwork through Chamber Music Ensemble Rehearsals

Two fundamental aspects of fostering positive teamwork are attentive listening and openness to diverse interpretations and experimentation. Observing a chamber music ensemble rehearsal offers valuable insights into these crucial traits. Performing artists are trained to listen to multiple voices simultaneously. While focusing on their own part and mastering their instrument, they must also be attuned to the melodic, rhythmic, and counterpoint elements from their fellow musicians.

When interpreting disagreements, the typical approach in artistic settings is to foster a language that promotes experimentation. Artistic performance is not about achieving a singular, fixed result but rather about exploring various interpretations. This perspective emphasizes that art is a continuous journey of exploration rather than a final, conclusive triumph.

Mei Lim, in his article in *Psychology of Music* (Lim, 2014), identifies four essential skills for successful ensemble players and vocalists: self-awareness, restraint, interpersonal awareness, and mutual sensitivity. These skills are also vital leadership attributes. By paralleling these disciplines, one can see how creativity and potential growth are nurtured in both fields.

Bathurst, in *Administrative Sciences* (Bathurst & Ladkin, 2012), argues that ensemble leadership should be viewed as a plural process that elevates all group members to achieve mutual goals. Vredenburgh and Yunxia, in *Business Horizons* (Vredenburgh & Yunxia He, 2003), discuss the Orpheus Chamber Orchestra, a renowned conductor-less ensemble from the 1970s. Orpheus employs a rotating team leadership structure, fostering shared influence and collaborative creativity. This approach leads to high organizational commitment and low turnover, emphasizing participative leadership, avoiding hierarchical control, and promoting shared decision-making.

Other disciplines could benefit from adopting this ensemble teamwork approach. Embracing multiple possibilities and allowing for diverse perspectives are key elements of a musical ensemble. Artistic endeavours

Artistic endeavours thrive on curiosity, experimentation, and accommodating various viewpoints, which can also enhance teamwork and leadership in other fields

thrive on curiosity, experimentation, and accommodating various viewpoints, which can also enhance teamwork and leadership in other fields.

C: Reverse Engineering of Success

At prestigious institutions like the Royal Academy of Music in London, the concept of "reverse engineering of success" has become a fundamental part of advanced music training. Following major recitals, students and mentors engage in reflective discussions to dissect what contributed to a successful performance, shifting the focus from merely analyzing failures.

This practice involves a systematic examination of both internal and external factors that impact a notable performance. Internal factors may include the sequence and presentation of pieces, preparation level, practice routine on the day of the concert, personal mood, dietary habits, meditation, and the cultivation of positive energy. External factors could encompass the type of instrument used, hall size, lighting, distance from the stage to the first row, audience characteristics, their familiarity with the performer and repertoire, and concert timing.

This meticulous and reflective approach is invaluable for performers, enabling them to connect more deeply with their audience and understand the multifaceted elements that contribute to their successes and failures.

By integrating emotional aspects into their analysis, performers can enhance their real-time engagement and performance quality.

The "reverse engineering of success" concept can be a model for other disciplines as well. By applying a similar level of scrutiny to their processes, organizations and leaders can gain a deeper appreciation of success, identify critical factors that drive performance, and foster a culture of continuous improvement and strategic growth.

D. The Power of Improvisation – Lessons from the Mind of a Performing Artist

Being a performing artist is not about playing it safe. The amount of preparation required to perform a piano piece like *Jeux d'eau* (Play of Water) by Maurice Ravel is immense. Although this piece lasts only five minutes, it demands a wide range of abilities: from complete command of the keyboard and extraordinary virtuosity to emotional sincerity and mastery of impressionistic style. Despite continuous daily practice of up to eight hours over months, a successful performance is never guaranteed. Even minor distractions, such as a phone ringing during a concert, can disrupt concentration and potentially lead to a perceived "failure." Therefore, it is crucial for performers to develop the ability to improvize within their style of playing. This skill is essential for any performer, whether in jazz or classical music.

However, improvisation is not just a skill or technique that can be professionally acquired; it is a state of mind. In his book *Free Play*, Nachmanovitch (1990) explains that while structure and practice provide a foundation for true improvization, one must also embrace mistakes and adopt a mindset that focuses on the creative process rather than merely on achieving a predefined end. He argues that outcomes become more meaningful and authentic when individuals immerse themselves fully in the process. Nachmanovitch identifies the "inner critic"— the voice of self-doubt and judgment—as a major obstacle to creativity. He encourages readers to silence this inner critic to allow creativity to flow more freely. Similarly, Green (1982), in *The Inner Game of Music*, introduces the concept of two "selves." Self 1 is the critical, judgmental voice that fosters doubt and hinders performance, while Self 2 represents the natural, intuitive part of the mind that performs tasks effortlessly when Self 1's interference is minimized. The goal is to quiet Self 1 and allow Self 2 to take control.

Although it is challenging, particularly for trained classical musicians (Ayerst, 2021), performers are often trained to continue live performances despite given mistakes. They cannot simply "go back" and restart

> **For true improvization, one must also embrace mistakes and adopt a mindset that focuses on the creative process rather than merely on achieving a predefined end.**

a piece when it does not align with their intentions in front of an audience. Rapid adjustment to new situations involves self-forgiveness, which is essential for delivering a memorable performance. It is not about achieving perfection in hitting the right notes at the right speed, but about playing with a personal touch. This emotional expression resonates with listeners long after the performance has ended.

Interestingly, the term used for engaging with a musical instrument is "play." Barry Green distinguishes between "gaming" and "playing" a musical instrument. We do not "game" the piano; we "play" it. This distinction emphasizes viewing musical performance as a form of play—characterized by enjoyment and natural expression—rather than a competitive or mechanical task.

The aim is to highlight the difference between a rigid, outcome-driven activity ("gaming") and an expressive, creative, and joyful experience ("playing").

Conclusion: Leadership as an Art Form

The lessons drawn from the performing arts—whether through conducting, ensemble rehearsals, reverse engineering of success, or the art of improvization—offer valuable insights for leaders across fields. Leadership, like music, is not merely about adhering to rules but embracing creativity, collaboration, and the courage to innovate.

Viewing leadership as an art form in today's dynamic and interconnected world allows for a richer, more nuanced approach. By adopting principles from the performing arts, leaders can create environments where creativity flourishes and individuals are empowered to make a lasting impact. The transformative power of leadership lies not just in strategic decisions but in the ability to inspire, engage, and connect with others, parallel to a compelling musical performance.

*A **fully** referenced version of this article is available from editor@ dl-q.com*

***Orit Wolf** is an international concert pianist, composer, poet, and lecturer. Her expertise lies in Music Communication, Leadership, and Innovation in practice, where she is involved internationally in Academia and Industry. She was appointed the first Artist in Residence at the Technion for 2022-2023 (Israel Institute of Technology). www.oritwolf.com*

IDEAS FOR LEADERS

Academic research in accessible and engaging bite-sized chunks

IDEAS FOR LEADERS

DO I BELONG HERE? MEASURING EMPLOYEE ORGANIZATIONAL BELONGING

KEY CONCEPT

Perceived *organizational belonging* is the feeling by employees and managers that they are accepted and respected for who they are and that what they have to say enhances productivity and an employee's intent to stay with the organization. A Temple University study identifies four OB scales Myself, Acceptance, Diversity Valued, and Connection that organizations can use to gauge OB among their people and create targeted programs to address low organizational belonging.

IDEA SUMMARY

With many companies facing increased challenges in attracting and keeping employees, employee engagement and commitment has become even more vital to organizational success than ever before. Recent research has emphasized the positive impact of "organizational belonging" (OB) on employee satisfaction and engagement. OB is defined as "experiencing an acknowledgment of one's talents, interests, and experiences" and finding in the organization "whole acceptance of one's self-expression of these."

The challenge for leaders is to measure organizational belonging. A study by Temple University's Fox School of Business, in collaboration with IT consultancy SWK Technologies, aimed to fill the gap by developing organizational belonging metrics enabling companies to accurately gauge employee OB.

After an exhaustive review of past research on organizational belonging, the research team created a survey package that included 27 survey items to measure OB attitudes and perceptions. These survey items took the form of statements, such as:

- When I am with people from my organization, I feel included.
- When I speak up at work, I feel my opinion is valued.
- Employees of different backgrounds interact well in our company.
- Management shows a commitment to meeting employee disabilities' needs.
- I feel comfortable with being myself at work.
- For each statement, survey respondents would indicate their agreement based on a 6-point response scale from 1 (strongly disagree) to 6 (strongly agree).

These 27 OB survey items were combined in the package with survey items about productivity, intent to stay, position level in the organization, and various demographic factors (age, gender, race, religion, political scale).

The final piece of the package was a single, open essay-type item: ""In a few sentences, please describe what it is that makes you feel that you are a part of, or belong to, this company (what factors contribute to your sense of belonging here)."

The survey package was sent to 150 employees in a business technology company and 45 employees in an accounting firm.

In analyzing the results, the researchers deleted 9 items that overlapped with others. Through further statistical analysis, the researchers were able to group the remaining 18 OB items into four categories, which became four new Organizational Belonging scales:

1. Be Myself included survey statements such as "knowing my feedback is heard (good or bad) from my manager" and "I feel my voice and opinions are sought out by others in the company."

2. Acceptance survey statements included "I feel that I am included and involved in things that help the company be successful" and "having a voice in our wonderful caring community regardless of position."

3. Diversity Valued group statements such as "there is a culture of mutual respect" and "a culture that encourages open communication and collaboration."

4. Connection statements included, "We are all in

it together, one voice!" and "I like the fact that the people I interact with look after one another."

The researchers then explored the correlation between the four OB scales and the two outcomes: productivity and intent to stay. They found that all four OB scale items positively impacted both productivity and intent to stay, with Be Myself having the most impact on productivity and acceptance having the most impact on intent to stay.

The data did reveal some marginally significant impact of demographic variables (gender, race, religion, political scale, and age) and organizational variables (organizational tenure and position level/role) on the four OB scales. For the demographic variables, the study showed that men tended to rate higher than women on the Acceptance and Diversity Valued scales, while Christians tended to rate higher than non-Christians on the Connection scale. For organizational variables, management tended to rate higher than non-management on Be Myself and Connection.

Correlating demographic and organizational variables to outcomes, the researchers found that non-management perceived themselves as more productive and had a higher intent to stay than management.

In sum, while the four OB scales can be marginally impacted by demographic and organizational variables, the study showed that the scales were distinct metrics that can be used to measure the level of organizational belonging felt by employees and managers of an organization

BUSINESS APPLICATION

Based on the study results, the researchers drew several important conclusions that can guide organizations in measuring and improving organizational belonging among their people.

- While all OB scales identified are significant, the most powerful of the four seems to be Be Myself. Allowing employees to express their opinions, even contradictory ones, without fear of retribution, and letting employees be their authentic selves are keys to building a sense of organizational belonging.

- The anonymous survey used in this study was valuable in surfacing demographic differences. However, to get responses from all employees including those who do not respond to surveys organizations should look for other discreet, data-gathering avenues, including focus groups and interviews. Feedback forums, such as department meetings and town halls, would allow even more employees to state their opinions.

- If demographic differences appear in perceived organizational belonging, the Human Resource Department should create programs that are specifically targeted to the needs of these groups. If women feel shut out of major decisions, for example, what steps can the organization take to increase a sense of belonging among female employees and managers?

REFERENCES
Organizational Belonging: Proposing a New Scale and Its Relationship to Demographic, Organization, and Outcome. Gary Blau, Daniel Goldberg, and Diana Kyser. Journal of Workplace Behavioral Health (February 2023). https://doi.org/10.1080/15555240.2023.2178448

Access this and more Ideas at ideasforleaders.com

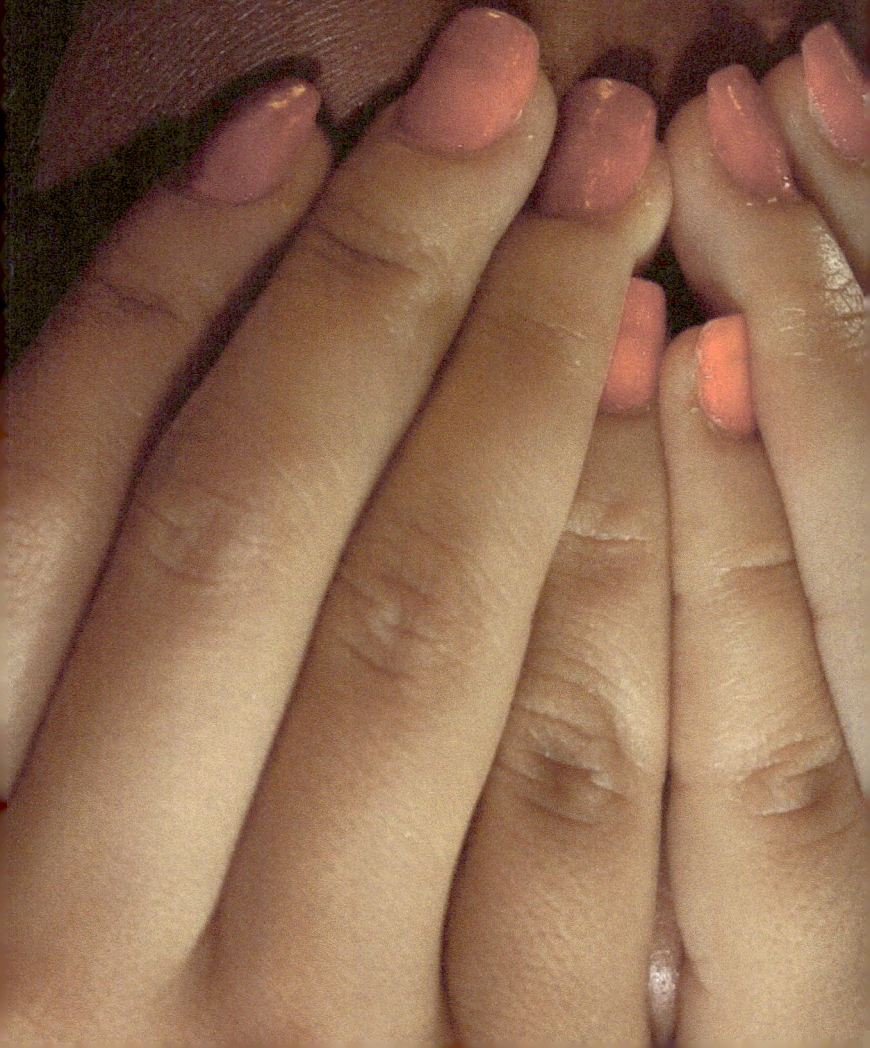
IDEAS FOR LEADERS

DON'T LET EMPLOYEES BECOME TOO INHIBITED TO DO THE RIGHT THING

KEY CONCEPT

The beneficial effect of our psychological inhibition system might be overstated. Research supported by multiple experiments show that a little inhibition goes a long way in helping people behave in socially acceptable ways. When the inhibition is too strong, however, the opposite may occur, as in the bystander effect.

IDEA SUMMARY

When we find ourselves in social situations that are unfamiliar, unsettling, or confusing, our tendency is not to react immediately, but rather to take a moment and think about what we want to do or say—that is, we appraise the situation to determine the appropriate behaviour in which to engage. As we appraise the situation, our behavioural inhibition system (BIS) is activated. The BIS helps us refrain from acting instinctively and without thinking.

The consensus is that the BIS prevents us from unthinkingly engaging in antisocial and destructive behaviour. For example, when we are frustrated, the BIS prevents us from overreacting or taking aggressive and impulsive action that can lead to negative consequences for us and the people around us. The BIS thus encourages positive social behaviour—what is commonly known in psychology as prosocial behaviour.

This consensus view is challenged by the research of University of Utrecht professor Kees van den Bos, Fuqua Business School professor E. Allan Lind and their colleagues. This research, spanning a number of years and involving multiple experiments, culminated in an appraisal-inhibition model that adds nuance to the effect of the BIS on prosocial behaviour.

According to this model, a weak BIS—allowing people to act with less inhibition—can lead to prosocial behaviour. In contrast, activating the BIS too strongly can have the opposite effect, blocking acceptable and encouraged social behaviour.

To conduct their research, van den Bos, Lind and their colleagues first developed and tested a method to weaken the BIS by having participants recall situations or circumstances in which they did not care about what others thought—that is, when they acted without the BIS inhibiting their behaviour.

With this method in hand, the researchers conducted a series of experiments involving different situations when individuals often act against their own personal prosocial values.

One example is the bystander effect. The

bystander effect involves a situation in which a person sees someone in need of help but is inhibited from acting because no one else present is stepping in to provide help. In the researchers' bystander effect experiments, participants were divided between the strong BIS and weakened BIS conditions. A bystander effect situation was created: in one experiment someone dropped a load of pens on the floor; in another, someone pretended to choke on a piece of candy. Participants who were in the weakened BIS condition were more likely to help the person who dropped the pens or was potentially chocking on a piece of candy than those who were in the strong BIS condition. In short, people who were less inhibited were more prosocial—a reversal of the consensus.

In another experiment, the researchers explored how participants would react to receiving an advantageous outcome, given to them by a person in authority, that was unfair to others. In this series of experiments, the unfair outcome took different forms—for example, unwarranted overpayment, or unfairly receiving a free iPod. In each case, the participants who were less inhibited were more likely to reject the unfair outcome (the prosocial reaction). Participants whose BIS was strongly activated, in contrast, were more likely to accept the unfair outcome even though they knew it was wrong.

Why, in these two situations, did a strong BIS activation block rather than encourage prosocial behaviour (helping people in need of people and rejecting unfair outcomes)? The reason is that strong activation of the BIS leads people to go along with situational demands. In the bystander effect situation, inhibited participants did not want to act differently from the other bystanders ignoring the person in need. In the unfair outcome situation, the inhibited person did not want to challenge the authority who was offering the unfairly advantageous outcome.

Another counterintuitive result of the research is the impact of disinhibition on relationships with peers. Prosocial behaviour includes connecting with one's peers. However, a strong BIS will inhibit an individual's attempt to relate to his or her peers. Reducing the BIS, the research shows, encourages individuals to reach out to peers and conform to the group's behaviours—although drawing a line at behaviours that go against their personal values. The researchers note that some individuals have different social values than the majority. These individuals are proself rather than prosocial, only caring about themselves and never caring what others think. The experiments relate to participants with prosocial values, whose lack of inhibition leads to prosocial behaviour because they are acting according to their personal values. Proself individuals acting in accordance with their personal values are going to act in antisocial ways. Uninhibited proself individuals, for example, are more than happy to keep the unfair outcome.

BUSINESS APPLICATION

Van den Bos, Lind, and their colleagues are quick to point out that further research is required to understand the full extent of benign disinhibition. They also don't discount the benefits of BIS. However, the research offers a warning to managers and organizations that oversimplifying the effect of BIS can lead to unintended consequences. To mitigate these consequences, managers and organizations can use the methodology of reminding their people of events in which they were not inhibited, thus eliciting reactions that are more aligned with their personal, prosocial values—and with the behaviour that the organization is seeking.

If, for example, an employee needs help, fellow employees should seek to help them regardless of what others are doing (i.e., overcoming the bystander effect). If a manager confers an unearned reward on an employee—for example, conferring credit to a team leader for a team member's work—that team leader should not be hesitant in setting the record straight.

The bottom line is balance: helping employees have enough control (inhibition) to take the time to act appropriately in unsettling situations without letting an overly strong BIS prevent them from acting according to their personal values.

Access this and more Ideas at *ideasforleaders.com*

WHAT'S LOVE GOT TO DO WITH WORK?

KEY CONCEPT

A culture of companionate love — defined as affection and compassion — in the workplace can lead to greater employee satisfaction and engagement, while a culture that undermines such emotions leads to unhappy workers... and customers.

IDEA SUMMARY

Love is not a word often found in management literature, although the consensus now recognizes the power of emotions in motivating (or demotivating) people. Daniel Goleman and others have popularized the influence of emotions in effective leadership. But even in discussions involving emotions, rarely does the word 'love' come up. Love in the workplace? Don't most companies have rules against such a thing?

New research shows that companionate love, defined as feelings of affection, compassion, caring and tenderness for others, can in fact impact employee morale and effectiveness. In organizations that featured a culture of companionate love — the research focused first on the health care industry — employees were more engaged, less emotionally exhausted, and more satisfied with their jobs, and worked better in teams. From the customer perspective — in this research, patients and their families — a culture of companionate love led to more pleasant moods (as assessed by staff), more satisfaction and a higher quality of life. The families of patients were also more likely to recommend the facility when such a culture existed.

While the health care field might be an industry in which companionate love can play a part, some might question its applicability to other industries. When the same research was extended beyond health care to more than 3,000 employees in other industries, the correlation between companionate love and employee and customer satisfaction was repeated. Not all industries showed the same level of companionate care although, surprisingly, the greatest range of companionate love occurred within industries rather than between industries. In some firms in the financial industry, for example, rated very low on companionate love, while others rated as high as any health care company.

Can there be too much companionate love? It's possible. If team members are too compassionate and caring, they may overlook unethical behaviour on the part of one of their members. This indeed happened when physicians in a group medical practice overlooked the accounting fraud of one of their own because of their compassion for him following a natural disaster that hit his home.

BUSINESS APPLICATION

While there may always be certain employees who are caring and empathetic, companionate love has a direct impact on employee and customer satisfaction (and thus reducing employee turnover and customer loyalty) when it is encouraged and nurtured as part of the organizational culture. Southwest Airlines, PepsiCo and Whole Foods (which has a set of principles that begin with 'love') are some of the larger companies that are not afraid to emphasize the importance of affection and caring as part of the values and principles of the firm. Look at your company's statement of principles and values: does the word 'love' or 'caring' appear? How does your statement of values and principles compare to the following statement from Zappos: "We are more than a team though...we are a family. We watch out for each other, care for each other and go above and beyond for each other."

Just as important, are such sentiments conveyed through the attitudes and behaviours encouraged and modelled by the leaders of the firm? Employees and managers will take their cues from the top. No matter what the mission statements might say, a culture is built through the actions of executives first.

It is important that emotional culture and cognitive culture are not mutually exclusive. Your organization can still emphasize results while encouraging caring and compassion. Both American Airlines and Southwest Airlines have a results – and achievement-oriented cultures, Southwest believe that expressing authentic emotions is the best way to build these results; for American Airlines, success comes from being the emotionally restrained 'stainless steel' airline.

REFERENCES
What's love got to do with it? A longitudinal study of the culture of companionate love and employee and client outcomes in the long-term care setting. Sigal G. Barsade & Olivia A. O'Neill. Administrative Science Quarterly (Forthcoming).

Access this and more Ideas at ideasforleaders.com

Book Reviews

More Human

How the Power of AI Can Transform the Way You Lead

By Rasmus Hougaard and Jacqueline Carter

*HBR Press; March, 2025; 208pp:
ISBN: 978-8-892-790-62-8*

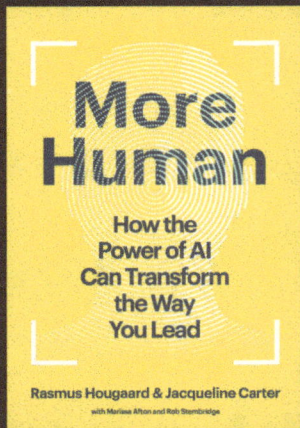

The authors, who have deep experience in human-centred leadership research, have been asking questions of senior leaders of large organizations to put this book and their thinking together — and make the claim it is 'the first research into leadership within the context of AI'.

However, as the authors' point out, AI's amazing abilities are only half the story, you have to be able to use them. As they say, 'you can own a Ferrari, and still be a bad driver' this book is their manual on how to manage yourself in relation to the promises and risks of AI. As AI transforms itself on a daily basis, the authors offer no specific tools to use, as they are instantly outdated – but they do offer a route map to more intentional development of leadership and new frameworks for balancing technology and humanness.

The initial premise is that AI can do three major transformative things for leaders:

- *Save time to enable greater focus on the individuals.* As an example, traditionally the collecting and collating of annual review data would take up much of the prep time for a review, no longer. So, use this time to think more about the individual than their review data, before the meeting.
- *Ultra-personalized leadership.* Every individual is unique, so leaders have had to adopt more catch-all approaches for large teams. With AI it can be much simpler to tailor personalized approaches.
- *Elevate the best of humanness.* Humans are irrational, chaotic, emotional – which is part of our magic, but it is also a weakness – both for leaders and those they lead. AI can be more czonsistent. The authors liken it to an exo-skeleton for our cognitive, emotional and social powers.

Augmentation (as DLQ's previous issue focused on) is the name of the AI leadership game. Hougaard and Carter support the view that we are entering the *Age of Augmentation*.

The AI-Augmented Leader, is one who can marry their use of AI with the authors' three core human-centred leadership qualities of Awareness, Wisdom and Compassion. With high levels of these three, leaders can assess context and identify relevant objectives and goals better (awareness); will ask better questions of the vast archive of knowledge AI holds and draws from and can better interpret its output (wisdom); and can weave together leading with their heart and using AI insights (compassion).

These three AI-augmented activities/capacities then, in the authors' vision, create a positive feedback loop, that will build better teams and organizational performance and outcomes.

The book is very easily read – and not long – and has the double advantage that it reaffirms many key aspects of human-centred leadership. The authors never let go of the central concept, that remaining human-centred, as the book title underlines, is THE most important capacity.

To lead well in the Age of Augmentation though we need to collaborate with the new technology as it emerges and evolves around us. Hougaard and Carter

focus in on two core practices. The first is to 'double-down' on your inner development. Their research highlighted that this inner development focus was too often considered a distraction by the AI hungry; but it remains the central pillar. You will never be a good leader without attending to your own mind. "An understanding of your own mind enables you to optimize your leadership potential and leverage the best of the AI tools and technologies at your disposal" they assert.

The second practice is to integrate AI into everything you do – from writing an email to asking what research to read on a topic. "Embrace how AI can augment your leadership by engaging it early and often in any leadership activity."

In many respects none of this is new – great leadership, especially human-centred leadership, has always been about combining a curious, systems-exploring mindset with a compassion for others, to create the best conditions for them to do their work in. AI brings a new level of best, for those conditions, and leaders need to leverage it.

Tribal

How Cultural Instincts That Divide Us Can Help Bring Us Together

By Michael Morris

Swift Press – Random House; November, 2024; 216pp; ISBN: 978-180-075-55-17-8

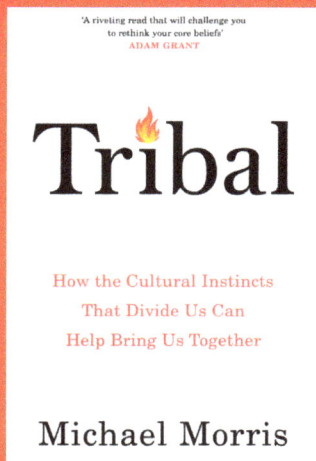

iving in a world that every day becomes a little more managed by artificial intelligence, begs all sorts of questions of what the future of organizations might look like. What is clear is that we humans are not likely to change radically in the things that drive us and shape our behaviours.

The context of the world around us, and the activities that impact our lives may change beyond all recognition over the next few decades, but humans will still be emotional creatures, subject to the physical limitations our bodies and minds are constrained by.

What seems probable is that our over-riding success characteristic that has brought us to this point in history,

REVIEW

our ability to collaborate, will still be key to how humanity operates, even if what we collaborate on is different to what we are used to.

Michael Morris is the Chavkin-Chang Professor of Leadership at Columbia Business School, and Columbia University's department of psychology. In this, his first, book Morris describes how humanity is shaped by three deep tribal instincts – and how we interpret those dictates how successfully or not we progress.

The tribal instincts are sideways-looking, upward-looking and backwards-looking: the *peer instinct*, the *hero instinct*, and the *ancestor instinct*. The weight and focus we put on each of these will mould how we perform individually and collectively.

All our tribal instincts, Morris asserts, are based on our special ability to observe others and adopt and adapt behaviours. Humans are distinct from our great ape cousins by having whites to our eyes – and this, he suggests, allows us to notice more easily where our companions are looking. If we can see our friend staring at a large fruit on a tree, that is useful information to have. Our gorilla, chimp and bonobo cousins would struggle to notice the same. And even if they did, they would be unlikely to adopt any successful methods to reach the fruit that they see their peers use.

This is key to our ability to learn, and in Newton's phrase, stand on the shoulders of giants, so progressing our knowledge. More importantly perhaps, it encourages us to conform; act in similar ways to the rest of the group.

We also tend to look up to the more powerful members of our societies to work out what they do, that has got them to their positions of influence. This 'hero' instinct is more debatable on its positive impact, your reviewer would suggest. Heroes are dangerous role models, they tend to see the world through an ego-centric lens (see Samir Selmanović's article in this issue). That said, Morris's definition of a hero is someone who acts selflessly for the benefit of the tribe – though they get recognition for that. This leads him to see the Hero instinct as being a 'prosocial' one.

The final instinct, the ancestor instinct, is a grounding one; where traditions and reverence for the past guides behaviours. He tells the extraordinary tale of the Ardeche cave where paintings were made by our ancient ancestors, 35,000 years ago; and then after a 29,000 year gap (presumed to be because the cave entrance became blocked) more paintings were made 6,000 years ago. The 'continuity of practice' instinct is deep seated within us, and makes rituals and traditions meaningful, even if logically pointless, and those who do them connected to the 'tribe'.

Peer instincts are prompted by tribal signals (the things we observe, and can use); Hero instincts by tribal symbols (things we observe, and create culture); and Ancestor instincts by ceremony. Ceremony is a way of bringing people together and importantly subsuming the individual in place of the collective – so harnessing a collaborative spirit.

The second part of the book looks at how the peer signals, hero symbols and ancestor traditions can be leveraged to change behaviour.

Signals are, in many ways, 'nudge' theory. Making people feel they should change in order to be more like their neighbours, colleagues or fellow citizens. Cialdini's tweaking of public messaging – whether that be tax returns or energy saved – to show how far from the norm individuals are. Conforming is comforting, and it is the signals that highlight how closely we are doing so that are important.

Symbols, are, it turns out, strikingly like signals, but from those with klout. Today we are surrounded by influencers, whose accoutrements and behaviours are symbols for their followers, whether than be Kim Kardashian's derriere or a Brazilian telenovela star's number of children.

Ceremonies, are easier to track and trace – though often just as manufactured – the Changing of the Guard

Leveraging the instincts is a subtle and nuanced skill, and will vary with every change challenge

at Buckingham Palace was instigated to create a sense of tradition. Hedge funds' 2 and 20% fee structure apparently derives form Phoenician sea captains.

In the third part of the book Morris sets out how these insights can be brought to create positive change in organizations. He provides two routes, a grassroots movement to build momentum, which relies on incremental steps that build trust with the community – whether that be on being more punctual in Ecuador, or abandoning female circumcision in Senegal. Or top-level diktat imposed from above – whether that be Sweden changing the side of the road it drives on, or Mayor Bloomberg outlawing smoking in bars. These latter examples worked as the community understood and saw the benefits; banning outsized soda cups failed, as it carried less impact to others, so the community aspects were lost.

Tribal instincts clearly work for good and ill – and today's world is much more tribally divided than a decade or two ago. How do we manage and de-escalate this, Morris asks?

We need to inspect the three instincts and assess their levels. 'Has peer instinct metastasized into group-think?'; has hero-instinct just morphed into trashing other's leaders and othering? Understanding where our instincts are at fault is the necessary first step. We need to use the opposing tribe's language to persuade them; and facts and evidence carry little weight, especially with the better educated, if it contradicts strongly held beliefs. Morris sees that to convince others, you need to be an individual first, not a tribal proponent.

Leveraging the instincts is a subtle and nuanced skill, and will vary with every change challenge. Creating new heroes and new rituals is part of the process; and realizing that, as humans, tribes may protect us, but we have always progressed faster and better when we collaborate.

Rich in stories but lighter on practical advice, this book opens our eyes to the root causes of current societal and organizational divides, and points to a pathway to tackle them.

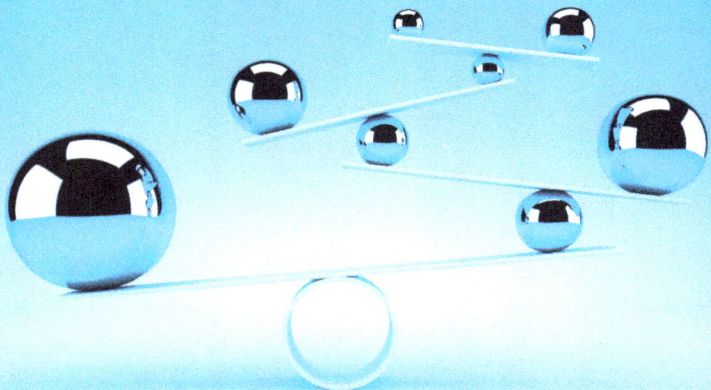

Balanced management begins with reflection

When do your mid-level managers have the chance to stop and reflect on their leadership practice?

Join our growing community of practice once a month for 30 minutes of provocation from a respected thought-leader and 40 minutes of breakout group discussion with other community members from a diverse range of UK organizations.

Upcoming speakers include **Dr Eve Poole on Leadersmithing**; **Prof Maja Djikic on the Possible Self**; **Rebecca Stephens on Stopping, Pausing and Reflecting** – plus enjoy other member benefits - including print copies of DLQ.

**For further details visit
uk.ideasforleaders.com**

SUSTAINABLE
LEADERSHIP
community

About the Publishers

Ideas for Leaders

Ideas for Leaders summarizes the thinking of the foremost researchers and experts on leadership and management practice from the world's top business schools and management research institutions. With these concise and easily readable 'Ideas' you can quickly and easily inform yourself and your colleagues about the latest insights into management best practice.

The research-based Ideas are supported by a growing series of podcasts with influential thinkers, CEOs, and other leading leadership and management experts from large organizations and small. We also publish book reviews and a new series of online programs.

www.ideasforleaders.com

The Center for the Future of Organization (CFFO)

CFFO is an independent Think Tank and Research Center at the Drucker School of Management at Claremont Graduate University. The Center's mission is to deepen our understanding of new capabilities that are critical to succeed in a digitally connected world, and to support leaders and organizations along their transformational journey.

In the tradition of Peter Drucker, the Center works across disciplines, combining conceptual depth with practical applicability and ethical responsibility, in close collaboration and connection with thought leaders and practice leaders from academia, business, and consulting.

www.futureorg.org

DLQ Advisory Board

DevelopingLeaders
Quarterly

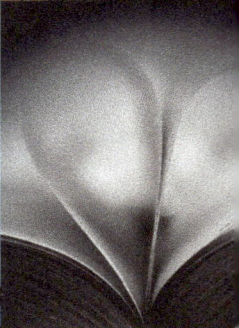